Pentecost Lost

---Don't Believe it!
A Call to Know Holy Spirit

Pat & Wayne Holland
www.patriciaholland.org

© Copyright 2011 Patricia Holland

All rights reserved. This book is protected under the copyright laws of the United States of America. This book may not be copied or reprinted for commercial gain or profit. The use of short quotations or occasional page coping for personal or group study is permitted and encouraged.

New Living Translation
Unless otherwise indicated, all Scripture quotations are taken from the *Holy Bible*, New Living Translation, copyright © 1996, 2004, 2007. Used by permission of Tyndale House Publishers Inc., Carol Stream, Illinois 60188. All rights reserved.

King James Version
Scripture quotations marked "KJV" are taken from the Holy Bible, King James Version, Cambridge, 1769.

New International Version
Scripture quotations marked "NIV" are taken from the HOLY BIBLE, NEW INTERNATIONAL VERSION ®. Copyright © 1973, 1978, 1984 by International Bible Society. Used by permission of Zondervan.

All rights reserved.
Please note that all nouns and pronouns used to reference God, Jesus, and Holy Spirit have been capitalized.

Also, please note that the name satan and related names are not capitalized in this book. We chose to violate grammatical rules by choosing not to acknowledge him.

For Worldwide Distribution
Printed in the United States of America
First Printing, 2011

ISBN 978-1-57817-000-5

Patricia Holland
Jacksonville, FL 32259
www.patriciaholland.org

Preface

I wish I could have this conversation with you - over a cup of really good coffee and one of my fresh-from-the-oven, cinnamon rolls - on the back porch overlooking the mountains. Maybe one day we will, but today, for the sake of convenience, we're meeting through the pages of this book. Thank you for giving me the opportunity to tell you about my dear friend, Holy Spirit.

You probably noticed I left off the article "the" when I mentioned His name. I'll do that throughout the book, not out of irreverence, but as a reminder that He is not a thing or an "it" but God, the third person of the Trinity. He is so special to me that often I call Him precious Holy Spirit.

In this book, I want to share my lifelong pursuit to know Him. I want to help you know Him better, love Him more, and experience Him more deeply. I want to talk with you. So, get comfortable, and by all means, grab yourself a cup of coffee, and let's talk.

ACKNOWLEDGEMENTS

I have been extremely blessed to have people in my life that have believed in me and have motivated and encouraged me to follow the leading of precious Holy Spirit during the writing of this book. I wish to provide special recognition to each of them:

To my wonderful husband Wayne for your patience and love as we have partnered to obey God in birthing this book.

To Pastor Ken Cramer for all your encouragement, insight and valuable suggestions during the whole process to get this book to print!

To my dear friend, Sue Combs, for all your words of encouragement and for being a wonderful sounding board.

To Cathy Exley for your invaluable recommendations and vivid insight.

To Jason Burns for the amazing graphic design of the book cover.

To my special editor, Barbara Iderosa of Best Editing, for taking the manuscript to the next level during the editing process. You have been a blessing from God.

DEDICATION

This book is dedicated to my precious grandchildren, Ashlyn, Brayden, Karyn and Keira. You bring so much joy to my life. I pray that you will walk in the fullness of God's plan for your life; a fullness available through the knowledge and power of Holy Spirit.

Introduction

What is the significance of Pentecost? Is it merely a historical event in the Jewish culture? What does Holy Spirit have to do with Pentecost? Are tongues of the devil? Was speaking in unknown tongues just for the disciples? Is Pentecost just too much trouble for us to understand?

There seems to be a menacing fence - complete with a huge "Keep Out" sign - surrounding Pentecost and its accompanying infilling of Holy Spirit. Religion says, "You receive all you need when you get saved." But Jesus told His disciples after His resurrection to "receive the Holy Spirit[1]." Instead of searching, discovering, and receiving Holy Spirit, we are content to leave that portion of the Bible boarded up and as far removed from our lives as possible. That choice robs believers of enjoying an incomparable relationship with Holy Spirit. Confused and frightened by the hounds of tradition and ignorance, far too many believers remain silent and powerless. Could the Person of Pentecost be the missing dynamo in the modern, anemic church?

Pentecost ignored is Pentecost lost. When we fail to embrace Pentecost, we forfeit its benefits. This decision robs believers of a vast gold mine of spiritual gifts that are available. Pentecost must be taught to be sought. Pentecost must be believed to be seized.

In this book, we will un-wrap the mystery of Pentecost using scripture, stories, and illustrations, so you can know Him well enough to understand and communicate that understanding more effectively to your family and friends. You will have word pictures and information to help you talk about Him more effectively with others.

In this book, we will look at seven biblical pictures that describe Holy Spirit. Each picture begins with the letter "P" to make them easy to remember: Pentecost-Calendar; Presence-Water; Present-Gift; Partnership-Wind; Passion-Fire; Purpose-Oil; Power-Electricity.

---

[1] John 20:22

Table of Contents

Chapter 1: Pentecost – Calendar 1

Chapter 2: Presence - Water 20

Chapter 3: Promised - Gift 37

Chapter 4: Partner - Wind 70

Chapter 5: Passion - Fire 108

Chapter 6: Purpose - Oil 135

Chapter 7: Power - Electricity 160

Chapter One

Pentecost- Calendar

Bonsai
While I agree bonsai trees are both beautiful and treasured, still I find them to be profoundly sad. Trees are designed to be big! You climb in them, swing on their branches, or rest in the shade of their bushy canopies. The bonsai trees are too small for any of those activities. Mature trees will reach heights of 50 to 150 feet, but a mature bonsai tree will only reach 12 to 14 inches. Bonsai trees are not dwarfed by genetics; they are miniature by deliberate design. The blueprint locked inside the DNA of the young seedling promises a mighty giant, but that destiny is deliberately altered to create a bonsai. To grow a bonsai, the taproot is clipped, and the branches are pruned. Then, the developing seedling is planted in a shallow container. The bonsai reaches maturity, but it never reaches its potential. The miniature lives in a shallow dish, while its giant relative grows unconstrained outside. Locked inside every bonsai is the unfulfilled potential to kiss the sky.

The reality that there are bonsai Christians goes beyond sad to heartbreaking. A bonsai Christian is the result of unrealized and unleashed potential—God-implanted potential. God's incorruptible seed was destined to produce believers who would be called "...trees of righteousness, the planting of the Lord, that He may be glorified" (Isaiah 61:3 KJV). You are called to be like a tall, magnificent tree, visually displaying the nature and glory of God. You are called to be like a giant sequoia, a tree of righteousness, so God can receive glory from your life. He doesn't get glory when you live your life chained and defeated by sin or stunted with tiny faith and miniature results. Too many believers live satisfied and content as bonsai Christians instead of being the giants God intended.

Pentecost Lost

The giant sequoias that grow in the Sierra Nevada Mountains are among the oldest and largest living things of the earth. The bark on these towering wonders is over 12 inches thick. A picture doesn't capture the enormity of the sequoia. These supersized giants are spectacular, reaching heights of 250 feet. When I stood at the base of the General Sherman tree, named for its exceptional stature, I commented to my husband, "Look how small the branches are." My husband read the sign to me: The lowest limb was so high that it appeared to be very small; yet, it was six feet, eight inches in diameter, more than the average man's height.[2] I felt like a tiny bug in comparison to their towering majesty.

Although God put the seed of potential in every believer to live super-sized Christian lives, too often we live like a bonsai with bonsai results. Something is missing. That something is actually "Someone." We are missing precious Holy Spirit.

Our unbelief has frozen Pentecost into a myth or a relic of the past, like a dinosaur. Whether by deliberate neglect, fear of the unknown, or skepticism, we have pushed Holy Spirit into a dark corner in the basement of our lives. Our inability to produce desired results leaves us questioning Him instead of questioning our beliefs and values. Oh yes, we have an abundance of activities, programs, and ideas - but no power. We have plenty of knowledge but little wisdom. We know how to compromise, organize, and economize, but we refuse to evangelize. Every believer has the DNA to be a spiritual king, but we have dropped the scepter and shirked away from the responsibility. We live as if Christianity was another self-help program, picking and choosing scriptures as though they were suggestions. We employ self-discipline to produce righteousness and holiness just as we would if we were trying various tips to stay on a diet. Our theology insists Holy Spirit exists, but divorced from His living presence, we live like deserted, hopeless orphans.

The early church was born in the fire and power of Holy Spirit. If the early church needed power, why don't we still need it? Did God

---

[2]www.nps.gov/seki/naturescience/sherman.htm/ (accessed May 27, 2011).

intend for the church to be born in a dynamic fire only to fizzle out? Or, has the lid of wrong teaching kept us from expecting and experiencing the infilling of Holy Spirit? Has unbelief cut our taproot, so we fail to reach for and receive the deep things of God? William Robinson Clark said:

> I believe that the cause of the general ignorance on this subject is that God will not reveal His fullness to a partially consecrated soul. Until our whole being is yielded to Him we cannot understand these things. God only reveals His fullness to those who are willing to go all lengths with Him.[3]

Let's dedicate our hearts to discover God's truth. What is the truth concerning Holy Spirit? We all have questions but some don't seem to have clear answers; others are simple to understand when you know where to look. Who is Holy Spirit? Do you receive Holy Spirit at the same time you receive salvation? Is there a second work of grace? Have tongues stopped? The truth is hidden in the seed of a mystery. Unlocking the mystery will enrich your life beyond your wildest dreams. In these seven lessons, I will take you on a journey through Scripture to unlock the mystery of Pentecost.

It's Like a Party

I love celebrations, even when we sing the birthday song off-key around the birthday cake. Celebrations give us a break from the drudgery of the routine and the ordinary. My favorite part of any celebration is the food. Everything tastes better when shared with friends. Some celebrations or festivals are pretty strange, like the following: The Pickle Festival in North Carolina; The Onion Festival

---

[3]William Robinson Clark, *The Paraclete: a series of discourses on the person and work of Holy Spirit* (Toronto, Canada, George N. Morang and Company, Limited: 1900), 33,
http://books.google.com/books?pg=PA33&dq=Holy+spirit&lr=&id=Swc3AA AAMAAJ&as_brr=4#v=onepage&q=&f=false (accessed April 3, 2011).

Pentecost Lost

in Georgia; or the Possum Festival in Florida. You must love onions a lot to have an Onion Festival. Groundhog Day is a very strange celebration. Who thinks a groundhog can predict the weather?

Every culture has unique celebrations. In the Jewish culture, there is a significant celebration called Pentecost or Shavuot (weeks). Pentecost, which derives its name from "Pente" (which means 50), occurs 50 days after Passover. While some of the Jewish celebrations are optional, every Jewish male was required to attend three annual feasts: Passover, Pentecost, and Tabernacle.[4] Pentecost was during the harvest season and lasted one day. While that may sound like a long party, some of the Jewish feasts lasted seven days. Let's look at each of these three feasts in the order of their occurrence to discover the meaning behind each celebration.

Passover Mystery

For four hundred years[5], the Jewish people were slaves in Egypt. In the desert, they made bricks and built buildings in the glaring, hot sun. Weary of the cruel oppression and servitude, the Israelites remembered God and began to pray. God responded by sending Moses, their deliverer, who arrived in Egypt with a staff in his hand, instructions in his head, and a promise in his heart[6]. As Moses obeyed the voice of God, amazing miracles followed. Pharaoh's hasty, harsh, hateful, and hard-hearted verdict would hatch his most horrible heartache. (Exodus 7-11) Try saying that three times really fast!

It was time for their evacuation, and God gave rigid instructions for their departure: prepare a Passover meal; kill a lamb; put the blood of the lamb on the doorposts of your house; pack your belongings; put on your traveling clothes; tie on your shoes; and eat your meal in a hurry. At midnight, the death angel would kill the oldest son in every household, except the houses where there was blood on the doorposts. In those homes, the oldest son would be

---

[4] Exodus 23:14
[5] Exodus 12:40
[6] Exodus 4:12

saved, because the death angel would see the blood of the lamb and "pass over" to the next home[7]. The Israelites carefully obeyed God's directives, and their households were saved from bitter loss and death. At midnight, death ripped through every other home whose doorpost was without the blood, killing the oldest son. Pharaoh's son was not exempt. Finally, Pharaoh groaned through bitter tears, "Get out!" And, they did. Passover, designed to become an annual event, commemorated the death angel passing over the blood of the lamb. (Exodus 12:6-42)

But there's still more to the story. God tucked a more powerful mystery into the picture of Passover. That mystery was unfolded and fulfilled many years later when Jesus, the Lamb of God, gave His life to pay the penalty of sin for all of mankind. Let's fast forward to the New Testament to see that mystery unfolded.

Jewish families celebrated Passover as outlined by Leviticus 23:15-22. They gathered in Jerusalem, remembering God's protection over their eldest sons in Egypt, and joyously celebrated together. Sacrifices were offered; old friends were reunited. They ate together. The ritual of the Passover meal, with all its symbolism, was repeated.

Just before His death, Jesus ate His last meal with His disciples at Passover. (Luke 22:15-20) There, He unfolded the mystery of Passover and changed its focus. From that point on, the focus of Passover was to remember Jesus, the sacrificial Lamb, every time they ate Passover. He compared His body to the bread that would be broken for them. He compared His blood, which would be spilled for them, to the Passover wine. Communion originates from the Passover meal, but Jesus moved the emphasis from an Old Testament memorial to a New Testament relationship.

Passover also celebrated the beginning of the barley harvest. As a reminder that God was the source of every good harvest, they were required to bring a bundle of grain to the priests. Before they brought the grain, they had to remove all the leaven or yeast from their homes. Yeast makes bread rise, and it is a symbol of sin in the Bible. This

---

[7] Exodus 12

activity illustrated their need to banish sin from their hearts. The bundle of wheat was lifted and waved as a wave-offering. This grain, without any leaven, is a picture of Jesus, who came to cleanse man from all sin. I thank God for giving us a picture to help us understand, but the picture is incomplete without Pentecost.

Old Testament Pentecost

The Israelites began their trek through a hot, dry, sandy desert. Each day was the same: gather personal things and walk; watch the children and walk; round up the straying sheep and walk. After 47 days of travel, Moses was visibly excited. God promised that He would bring him back safely to this exact place, and finally they had arrived. The people watched and rested as Moses climbed a mountain alone. They didn't have a clue what was about to happen. It was unimaginable that God would actually talk to them!

Cell phones have transformed our scope of communication. Wherever you are, as long as the area has coverage, you can be reached instantly with a call or a text message. God had exciting news to share with His servant on the top of that mountain in the desert, but He didn't need a cell phone. "Now if you obey me fully and keep my covenant, then out of all nations you will be my treasured possession. Although the whole earth is mine, [6] you will be for me a kingdom of priests and a holy nation." (Exodus 19:5-6)

God revealed His love with a promise to make them His treasured possession and a kingdom of priests. Don't miss God's conditions, *"If you obey me and keep my covenant..."*

What does it mean to be a kingdom of priests? God intended that each person would serve as a priest, ministering to God and people. A priest ministers upward to God (through worship) then outward to help people know and love God. God's loving provision enabled them to possess a land with everything they needed to live fruitful, happy lives. In their role as priests, they were to become agents of change, resulting in the inhabitants of the land serving the one true God.

Their preparation was essential. Boundaries or rules to govern their actions and a structured worship that would produce holy people who loved God had to be instituted. They stood on the brink of a new era. God had a plan, and it was time to turn the page of history. God was about to reveal Himself to an entire nation.

God explained the physical and spiritual preparation that was necessary for the God Encounter, which would occur in three days. Clean clothes and a good bath are a big deal when you don't have running water or a bath tub. They obeyed and got ready. Scrubbing between their toes and pulling on clean, scratchy, sun-dried clothes was more than dressing up for a special occasion. It was an activity of consecration and obedience that honored God.

On the third day, God showed up! The ground shook. Fire kissed the mountain top with the Shekinah Glory of God. The mountain smoked. The noise grew louder and louder. The meeting with God was spectacular and terrifying. The descriptions resemble a volcano.

A voice from the fire spoke clearly and distinctly to them. Everyone heard it. It was God's voice speaking their language, aloud. "And God spoke all these words..." (Exodus 20:1 KJV)

It is important to notice their travel time was forty-seven days; after that, their preparation was three days. The total time from Passover was exactly fifty days - or Pentecost.[8] Two revolutionary things took place at the Old Testament Pentecost: God gave them the Ten Commandments (or the Pentateuch), and they experienced His manifest presence. They heard the Word of God and experienced the presence of God. He was offering them the tools they needed to be a nation of priests.

God gave them a choice, and their response would be crucial. They could choose God's way or the way of natural reasoning. How did they respond? They were terrified by the supernatural, so they backed away. I wonder if they grabbed Moses' sleeve as a group gathered

---

[8]M.G. Easton M.A., D.D., *Illustrated Bible Dictionary*, Third Edition, (Thomas Nelson, Limited:1897) http://www.biblestudytools.com/dictionaries/eastons-bible-dictionary/pentecost.html (accessed May 27, 2011)

Pentecost Lost

around him, muttering in short, and frantic sentences something like this: "Moses, we're scared! From now on, you tell us what God has to say. We'll listen to what you say. Just ask God not to talk to us anymore. We're afraid that we might die." The rest of the people must have nodded their heads and clamored in agreement with this group.

Their commitment was brief. While Moses was on the mountain, the people worshipped a golden calf.[9] Now, instead of becoming priests, they needed one.

In spite of their fear and rebellion, God didn't want them to forget what they had experienced and been given. He instituted Pentecost as an annual Jewish holiday to remind them. This feast celebrated both the giving of the law and the end of the wheat harvest. In addition to the animal sacrifices, they were required to bring two loaves of bread - not raw grain, like that required at Passover - but loaves of bread, baked with leaven.

Why would God have them bring an offering containing leaven if leaven symbolized sin? Another secret is about to be unraveled. The bread they brought to God was a picture of the Church. The Church would not be perfect. It would be filled with people of varying degrees of commitment and consecration. Their imperfections could never diminish His love. His plan was to fill the church with His abiding presence and to cleanse it. Sin should not be something we try to hide or something that will hinder us from coming to God. Sin loses its hold in His presence. The Church was born at Pentecost.

Pentecost-Personalized

Although the Jewish people had celebrated Pentecost for hundreds of years, they only understood half the picture. God had more for them. It was a picture that Jesus would bring into clearer focus for both Jews and Gentiles.

Jesus explained to His disciples. "I am going away. But don't be sad." [10]

---

[9] Exodus 32

Did He say, "Don't be sad"? Their minds must have bristled with alarm. It sounded ridiculous! Jesus was leaving, and He told them to not be sad!

Jesus explained and promised that He would send Holy Spirit after His ascension to Heaven. Don't miss what Jesus was saying. Did you see two very important clues to unlock the mystery of Pentecost?

First, Jesus was limited by His physical body to occupy one place at a time. He could only teach and touch a limited number of people. Holy Spirit would not have those limitations because He was not clothed with a human body. He could be everywhere and anywhere.

Secondly, the disciples enjoyed a great friendship with Jesus. But, Holy Spirit would be more than a visitor. He would live inside them as a constant companion - teaching, guiding, talking, and loving. He could be with them anytime and anywhere. A deeper relationship would be available when Holy Spirit arrived.

New Testament Pentecost, which occurred 50 days after the crucifixion, opened the door for believers to move into a new dimension in their relationship with God. This new dimension would change the way believers live as much as telephones changed the way people communicate. Pentecost would change a believer's attitude and actions. Receiving the Person of Pentecost would affect all aspects of life. Holy Spirit would take each believer's living, being, and serving to a brand new level—a new dimension. He would enlarge a believer's capacity to know and serve God, much like a balloon remains stretched after it has been blown up.

Let me try to explain one aspect of the new dimension Holy Spirit would open for a believer. As we have already discussed, the Old Testament Pentecost celebrated the giving of the Ten Commandments. While Moses was still on the mountain with God, the Israelites constructed and worshipped an idol, which broke one of God's laws. Breaking God's law is sin. Jesus came to pay the ultimate price for our sins; that is redemption. The Book of Hebrews reveals God's ultimate plan as being both redemptive and regenerative. But,

---

[10] John 16:5-14

Pentecost Lost

this time, God would not write His laws on tablets of stone. Holy Spirit would write them on the hearts of His people. Those laws would be remembered and obeyed out of a heart of love that is energized by The Dynamo, Holy Spirit, resident in every Spirit-filled believer. Jesus testifies to us about this. First he says: "This is the new covenant I will make with my people on that day, says the Lord: I will put my laws in their hearts so they will understand them, and I will write them on their minds so they will obey them." (Hebrews 10:16) Ezekiel prophesied this event, which would affect a change so great that, instead of obeying out of a string of stringent laws, our love for Him would energize our obedience.[11]

Here are some clues for you to think about. At the Old Testament Pentecost, God gave the Word. The New Testament Pentecost enabled believers to understand and obey that Word. Jesus is the Word made flesh, and He is revealed to all through the infilling of Holy Spirit. One of the primary jobs Holy Spirit was sent to do is help all to know Jesus better. "All that the Father has is mine; this is what I mean when I say that the Spirit will reveal to you whatever he receives from me." (John 16:15)

Some movies are filmed in three dimensions, which add to the viewing experience. Not only are new movies being produced with three-dimensional technology, but movie makers are remaking old classics with this technology. The difference between two and three dimensional viewing is amazing. This is what the Person of Pentecost came to do for you. He wants to engage you in a new adventure. He wants to take the scripture, help you understand what it means, then give you the ability to live out what you see.

Pentecost Infilling

Easter baskets filled with coloring books, toys, and candy are special treats for little children. But, for me, personally, forget the extra stuff; just give me the chocolate bunny. I don't like the solid bunnies, because they are too hard. I prefer a good quality, real

---

[11]Ezekiel 36:23-27

chocolate, hollow bunny. Yet, I have learned from experience to be very careful when I pull the bunny out of the box. The fragile, chocolate bunny collapses easily because it is hollow.

Unlike chocolate bunnies, believers should not be hollow. With the arrival of Holy Spirit at Pentecost, believers can and should be filled to overflowing. He came to fill believers. When He fills us, we don't cave in to temptation or fear. His presence gives us strength to face obstacles.

There seems to be an innate underlying awareness of hollowness that people try to fill with things: popularity, wealth, and self-gratification. This is like trying to fill your chocolate bunny with toilet paper. Not too appetizing, is it? Chocolate bunnies weren't made to be stuffed with paper. Temporal feelings and possessions cannot fill the hollow place in your life. Stuff is fine. God wants you to enjoy stuff, but only to the extent that it enriches your life, not fills it.

Also, there seems to be an innate awareness in the heart of believers that God has more for us. Over the years, I have noticed some children responding repeatedly to the salvation invitation. While a child can be immature or misunderstand the invitation, I think in their hearts they knew God had more for them. I don't think this feeling is limited to children. God wants to give all of us more. We can all be filled with Holy Spirit.

In Acts 1:4 (KJV), Jesus issued a reminder and a reassurance, "Wait for the promise of the Father." After three years of intensive, hands-on mentoring, they still lacked one essential component: they needed to be filled with Holy Spirit. It wasn't enough for them to see the miracles or know the teachings of Christ. They needed more. To do the works of Christ required that Holy Spirit indwell and empower them. If the disciples needed Holy Spirit, then this generation needs Him, too! We need His sustaining presence today! Samuel Chadwick says:

> The Christian religion begins in a New Birth in the power of the Spirit. It is developed under His guidance, and sustained by His

presence; the power to attract is in attractiveness, and it is useless to advertise the banquet if there is nothing to eat.[12]

Pentecost Energized

Strategically, on the day of Pentecost, as promised, Holy Spirit arrived. His glorious and powerful introduction was supernatural. Tongues of fire, sounds of a mighty wind, ordinary people energized and equipped for extra-ordinary acts, and speaking in unknown languages; hardly begins to describe this event. The amazed crowds stopped when they heard Galileans praising God in their language; they realized it was a language that was unknown to these Galileans. The first church was born that day. It was born in the fire of Holy Spirit. They would become "God's Power and Light Company" on the earth because they tapped into the energy of heaven.

Look at the events of Exodus 19 and Acts 2.

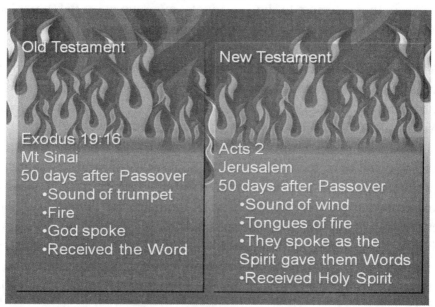

Old Testament
Exodus 19:16
Mt Sinai
50 days after Passover
• Sound of trumpet
• Fire
• God spoke
• Received the Word

New Testament
Acts 2
Jerusalem
50 days after Passover
• Sound of wind
• Tongues of fire
• They spoke as the Spirit gave them Words
• Received Holy Spirit

---

[12] Samuel Chadwick, *The Way to Pentecost,* (Light and Hope Publications, Berne, Indiana, Limited:1937), 5, http://wesley.nnu.edu/wesleyctr/books/0401-0500/HDM0496.pdf (accessed June1, 2011)

Look at the similarities between the two accounts. The New Testament Pentecost is the Old Testament Pentecost personalized. God was launching a new entity: the church - the body of believers. They would need new power and an indwelling presence of God to accomplish their mission.

We have solar lights in our yard. There are no electrical wires running to the lights. The lights are powered by a solar panel on top of each light. It collects energy from the sun to recharge the batteries. Amazing technology! My lights come on automatically at dusk and burn all night long. Then, the batteries are recharged the next day. With sufficient sunlight to recharge the battery, I will always have light at night!

The power of Pentecost is the living presence of Holy Spirit in your life. Worship and prayer provide an atmosphere for His manifest presence that energizes you to shine for Christ. Life in the Spirit enables you to overcome sin. Life in the Spirit recharges you to fulfill your God-given destiny at work and at home.

Pentecost is not a frozen glacier to visit and observe. Pentecost is not an extinct, terrifying dinosaur to fear or ignore. Pentecost is experiencing and receiving the Person of Holy Spirit. Pentecost is designed to be a living dynamo - the power generator - inside each believer. Pentecost is the fulfillment of God's promise to send precious Holy Spirit to become a resident inside believers. He comes with the assignment to reveal Jesus and empower you with a blazing passion that radiates the love of Christ to the lost.

You face a personal choice; the same choice was faced by the Israelites at the first Pentecost and again at the New Testament Pentecost in Jerusalem. Will you receive or refuse Him? If Pentecost is not a blazing fire on the altar of your heart, it can be. Precious Holy Spirit can change a frozen, historical Pentecost to a personal, living experience when you receive His infilling personally.

Pentecost Personified

Pentecost is dramatically more than an event. It is the giving of Holy Spirit. At Christmas, we celebrate the birth of Christ into this world, although we see glimpses of His presence in the Old Testament. "He was in the world, and the world was made by him, and the world knew him not." (John 1:10 KJV) We celebrate Christmas because God sent His Son into the world as a little baby, clothed in humanity, to be born in a Bethlehem stable. "So the Word became human and lived here on earth among us. He was full of unfailing love and faithfulness. And we have seen his glory, the glory of the only Son of the Father." (John 1:14) The descent of Holy Spirit at Pentecost was a unique event in the history of the world. We see His activity and power throughout the Old Testament, beginning at Genesis, but only as a visitor and then only for specific people or situations. Although we see Him empowering individuals in the Old Testament, Pentecost was the date of His introduction to the world as "The Promise" and "The Gift" for every believer. St. Augustine clarifies it: "He was now to come no longer as a transient Visitor, but as an eternal inhabitant."

William Robinson Clark encourages us to understand:

> Pentecost was as necessary to the Church and to the world as Christmas Day. If man needed to know God manifest in the flesh, the High Priest of Humanity, he no less needed the presence of Him who dwells in the body of the Church, and in the heart of the Christian, to illuminate, to purify, to enliven, to strengthen, and to comfort; to lead into all truth in thought and word and deed.[13]

If the symbol of Christmas is a tree or a star, then the symbol of Pentecost is fire. Don't miss the ramifications of that moment in Jerusalem. A fire would begin in the hearts of believers that would

---

[13]Clark, *The Paraclete*, 55.

turn the world upside down! The prophets said it would happen. Joel prophesied that Holy Spirit would be poured out on men, women, sons, and daughters in the last days. He saw not only the initial outpouring but the flood gate of gifts that the original infilling would initiate. He saw that prophecy, visions, and dreams would come as a result of the Spirit's outpouring in a believer's life. At Pentecost, Peter affirmed that this event was exactly what Joel said would happen.[14] It was a pivotal event that resulted in the conversion of three thousand believers.

Pentecost- Second Work of Grace

Being filled with Holy Spirit is a second work of grace, separate and distinct from being born again. A believer receives a measure of Holy Spirit when he receives Jesus as his Savior, but being baptized with Holy Spirit is a separate experience. We see the law given on the mountain. We see the living Word, Jesus, clothed with a body, arriving on the pages of humanity in the New Testament. We need the living Word, Jesus, to give us the new birth, making us a child of God.

Jesus explained the change that takes place in a sinner after repentance with a metaphor in Mark 2:22: "And no one puts new wine into old wineskins. The wine would burst the wineskins, spilling the wine and ruining the skins. New wine needs new wineskins." I struggled over the meaning of this verse for a long time.

First, what is a wineskin? In the arid regions where the Bible was written, the nomadic people used every part of an animal, much like the Native American Indians. That included the skins of cows, sheep, and goats, which were scraped and stretched to make a variety of useful items, including bags or containers. Sometimes, the entire skin of a goat was tied off to form a bag and used like a bottle to hold the grape juice from wine making. As the wine fermented, it would puff up in the bag, like yeast bread rises in a pan. Because a new skin is

---

[14] Joel 2:28,29

soft and flexible, it can stretch as the wine creates little bubbles. An old, tough, brittle wineskin will burst and spill the wine.

As sinners without Christ, we are like old wineskins. We cannot be a container for Holy Spirit until we receive Christ as our Savior. Believing on Jesus changes us. "Old things are passed away; behold, all things are become new." (2 Corinthians 5:17 KJV) We become a soft, new wineskin, but the metaphor continues. The wineskin needs to be filled with new wine.

Christ's redemptive story continues with His ascension and instructions not to leave Jerusalem until they had received Holy Spirit. Historically, the majority of churches have been satisfied to experience only the truth of Jesus, the living Word. They fail to embrace the second step, New Testament Pentecost, the infilling of Holy Spirit.

Reader Harris, from the early 1900's, said:

> Be filled with the Spirit. This is a command of God, as binding as any in the Decalogue: but a command that is to-day, to a great extent, ignored. Thank God, though, for the signs of revival of the spirit of enquiry all over the world. Thank God for the question which is agitating the Church to-day: " Is there a second DISTINCT WORK OF GRACE after conversion, and if so, what is it?" This is the question of questions. Satan has cheated nine-tenths of God's people out of this great big blessing; a blessing that would not only make them happy, but also effective for God. I believe it to be the will of God that all who know and experience this mighty blessing of the filling of Holy Spirit, should not be slow to declare it![15]

Samuel Chadwick gives his personal testimony of receiving God's second distinct work of grace:

> I owe everything to the gift of Pentecost. It came to me when I was not seeking it. I was about my Heavenly, Father's business, seeking

---

[15]Reader Harris, *When He is Come*, (Andrews Brothers, 1897) 46.
http://books.google.com/books?id=Hf0OAAAAQAAJ&pg=PR4#v=onepage&q&f=false (accessed June 1, 2011)

means whereby I could do the work to which He had called and sent me, and in my search I came across a prophet, heard a testimony, and set out to seek I knew not what. I knew that it was a bigger thing than I had ever known. It came along the line of duty, in a crisis of obedience. When it came I could not explain what had happened, but I was aware of things unspeakable and full of glory.

Some results were immediate. There came into my soul a deep peace, a thrilling joy, and a new sense of power. My mind was quickened. I felt that I had received a new faculty of understanding. Every power was vitalized. My bodily powers were quickened. There was a new sense of spring and vitality, a new power of endurance, and a strong man's exhilaration in big things. Things began to happen. What we had failed to do by strenuous endeavor came to pass without labor. It was as when the Lord Jesus stepped into the boat that with all their rowing had made no progress, "immediately the ship was at the land whither they went." It was gloriously wonderful.[16]

Jesus was born into this world through a supernatural activity of Holy Spirit. He did not begin His ministry until He had experienced the work of Holy Spirit at the Jordan River when Holy Spirit descended on Jesus during His baptism. Jesus was modeling more than water baptism; He was showing the importance of being filled with the Spirit. If Jesus needed Holy Spirit, then we need Him, too.

During the first revival after Pentecost, we see the new church operating under a new paradigm. Their actions revealed that there was a new emphasis on believers being filled with the Spirit, not just being born again. Phillip went to Samaria[17] and preached Jesus. Many people were converted. When the amazing revival news reached the Church at Jerusalem, they sent Peter and John to the new converts at Samaria. Their job was to teach and pray with the new converts to help them receive Holy Spirit.[18]

---

[16] Samuel Chadwick, Way to Pentecost p.17
[17] Acts 8:5
[18] Acts 8:14

DUI?

The crowd, gathering in response to the events of Acts 2, was both astonished and confused. What was happening? Why were these people acting so crazy? How was this event explained?

Like a policeman spotting an erratic driver and pulling him or her over to investigate a possible DUI, one spectator in the crowd suggested, "They're all drunk." Peter explained they were not drunk, yet he issued the first DUI. He explained that the things they saw were all Deeds Under the Influence; not under the influence of wine, but under the influence of Holy Spirit. Peter's list of DUIs began on Pentecost and continued throughout his ministry.

Let's look at some of them. At Pentecost, three thousand people were converted. Then, at the gate Beautiful, the lame man was healed. Countless miracles of all varieties were experienced. So many miracles took place that people would lay their loved ones along the street, expecting Peter's shadow to bring healing.

But, Peter wasn't the only one with DUIs. The book of Acts is called the Acts of the Apostles. Perhaps a better title would be the Acts of Holy Spirit. The believers in Acts were only conduits for precious Holy Spirit to flow through. God is using conduits in the earth today, so DUIs can be issued that bring Him glory. Every believer should demonstrate God's love and power with DUIs. I must warn you, we will not see Deeds Under the Influence unless we learn to "Dwell Under the Influence." That means that we must learn and practice spending time in God's presence. We must allow His love to penetrate our will and emotions to the point that it influences our attitudes and actions. Our focus in this book will be to Dwell Under the Influence, so we can have Deeds Under the Influence.

Pentecost - Calendar

Think about it:

DUI: Dwell Under the Influence

Dear God, What do you want me to take away from this chapter?

Did I receive a fresh revelation of Pentecost?

How will I allow that fresh revelation to be reflected in my life?

Chapter Two

Presence - Water

The Springhouse

It was hot, even in the shade. I still had a long distance to walk when I noticed the sign, "Springhouse Well." I hadn't seen an artesian well for years; maybe since my childhood. The sign reminded me of a visit to my aunt's house in rural Alabama. My dad had taken me to an artesian well on her property, where the water bubbled up into a small pool. I remember cupping my hands and drinking the coldest, most refreshing water I had ever tasted.

That memory made me even thirstier, so I quickened my steps, desperate to find the well. I could see the springhouse, small and quaint, across the parking lot. Water, refreshing and cold, was just what I needed on a scorching hot day like this one. The door squeaked on its hinges as I opened it and peered inside. The well was capped. I looked around for a hand-pump or faucet, but none was in sight. No water…only a sign to mark the place where people had once drank. Disappointed, I stepped back outside. The springhouse was beautiful, but beauty wasn't going to refresh me or satisfy my thirst. I left the springhouse as thirsty as I had come.

Our modern culture craves fresh, living water. God has lavishly supplied a crystal clear riverhead in the heart of the Church; still, our culture desperately attempts to quench their thirst from religious mud puddles. Could part of the problem be that the riverhead is dammed up and diverted, so it does not flow out of the Church? You cannot answer for the Church at large, but you can answer for yourself. Is living water flowing out of you?

Presence - Water

Water in the Desert

Have you ever sung "London Bridge is falling down, falling down..."? Did you know the London Bridge is now located in the middle of the Arizona desert? I had to see it!

The 167 mile drive between Las Vegas and Lake Havasu was lackluster. At first, I enjoyed the mountains, but then everything began to look much the same. As we traveled up and down the hills through the bleak desert, our eyes grew bored. There wasn't much to see unless we got out of the vehicle and looked closely for signs of life, such as bird or animal tracks. The road seemed to continue on and on with only an occasional road sign or small town to break the monotony. The same scenery was everywhere - rocks, lots of rocks...and cactus, the prickly, painful variety of cacti - dotting the roadside. Occasionally, we were entertained by a swift road runner darting past.

Why would anyone plop the London Bridge in the middle of the desert? The how and why of the London Bridge relocation story is fascinating.

The Colorado River is a major, life-sustaining source of water for both industrial and private utilization by people living in the arid American southwest. Spring rains and melting snow flooded the Colorado River. To prevent this flooding, produce power, and divert water into areas that didn't have adequate supplies, a series of five dams was built on the river.

One of these five dams is the Parker Dam. It is the deepest dam in the world. These dams produced lakes, one of which is called Lake Havasu. These dams and lakes brought life to the desert, creating peaceful, beautiful places. Birds and people splash in the cool, refreshing water, oblivious to the heat. Wildlife is abundant and varied. Noisy waterfowl feed among the cattails. A camera-shy family of partridges waddles across the parking lot to hide. The lake bustles with activity. Boating, fishing, swimming, and skiing have brought families to the lake. This area had been only a bleak desert, but water had transformed it into a lush paradise and habitat for wildlife.

Pentecost Lost

Robert McCulloch, owner of the McCulloch Chainsaw Manufacturing Company, fell in love with the beautiful, blue waters of Lake Havasu. It would be an amazing place to expand his business and build a city. In 1963, Mr. McCulloch purchased 26 square miles of barren desert at $75 an acre. His business expansions brought people to the city, but growth was slow.

While searching for ideas to entice growth, Mr. McCulloch read that the London Bridge was for sale. An article explained that the old bridge, which was too small for the city, was sinking in the Thames River. The city of London wanted to sell the bridge and replace it with a larger one. Mr. McCulloch was convinced the London Bridge was the magnet that would draw people to his infant city. He purchased the bridge for $2,460,000.00. It was taken apart; every stone numbered, and shipped to Lake Havasu, where it was meticulously reassembled on dry land. A channel was dug under the bridge to bring water from Lake Havasu. Mr. McCulloch profited from the beautiful transformation water had made in the desert.[19]

Holy Spirit does in the heart of an individual what water does to a desert. He transforms and brings life. That's what Jesus did. That's what precious Holy Spirit wants to do through believers today.

The desert terrain is barren and bleak. Sometimes, as you drive through the desert, you will see something different off in the distance. Perhaps you will squint to see clearer. You can see trees, tall and majestic. Approaching them, you can differentiate between the cottonwoods, chubby sycamore, and scraggly shrubs. The green foliage is radiant against the clear, blue sky.

Why the sudden change in the landscape? You can't see it yet because you're not close enough. But, it's there. You know it is because you see signs of life. As you approach, you catch a quick glimpse of it through the cattails, swaying under the weight of a black cowbird. Finally, you see life-giving water coursing through the desert. It's a fact; where water goes, life grows. Water is a change agent. Water unlocks the potential in a seed.

---

[19] http://en.wikipedia.org/wiki/Robert_P._McCulloch (accessed June 1, 2011)

Holy Spirit brings similar change in a life where He is welcomed. Life is sustained. Growth is initiated. When you welcome and anxiously crave His manifest presence in your life, change will come...life will come. Some of the change is glorious, but some is painful.

Jesus promised living water: "He that believeth on me as the Scripture hath said, out of his belly shall flow rivers of living water." (John 7:38 KJV) What a remarkable promise. The fulfillment of this promise is Holy Spirit. Like a natural river brings life, the river of Holy Spirit brings life. His presence is teeming with life-enriching benefits, such as joy, wisdom, and power. His presence germinates the seeds of your talents and also the seeds of the Word of God that has been deposited in you.

Although rivers have amazing power and purpose, they can be dammed up and diverted. You must choose the river or the desert. The areas in our life where we push God out begin to languish and die. In the areas where He fills and flows, life flourishes and thrives. His presence brings peace. His presence brings power to overcome sin. His presence produces abundant life, not ordinary life. This abundant life is for sharing, not hoarding.

Hugh Latimer points out, "The drop of rain maketh a hole in the stone, not by violence, but by oft falling." Too often we want a quick fix, an instant cure; but, so many answers come only as we spend time on a regular basis acquiring His wisdom and His ability to live our everyday lives. By welcoming and allowing the presence of Holy Spirit to flow in your life on a regular basis, you will experience the change and the growth that doesn't come any other way.

I Want Water

After miraculously crossing the Red Sea, the Israelites rested in Rephidim, which means a place of rest.

The Israelites, God's chosen people, existed in the wilderness, or desert: a harsh, dry environment. This desert had lots of rocks; they came in all sizes and shapes, from big boulders to the smaller gravel

Pentecost Lost

that crunched under their feet and wiggled between their toes as they walked. Only special plants designed by God to use a minimum of water or rest in a dormant state until the refreshing spring rains arrived could live there. But, the people who traveled there, unlike the desert plants, required water; but, there was no water in Rephidim. It's hard to rest when you're thirsty.

Modern culture has a hard time understanding the depths of this problem. When we get thirsty, we turn on a faucet, splashing and spilling and wasting as much water as we drink. Although their very lives depended on finding water, they didn't have a faucet or a well or even a store to buy water. So, what did they do? They did what people who don't live by faith almost always do…they complained. They complained to themselves and each other. But, loudest of all, they complained and blamed Moses.[20]

Moses responded very differently to the dearth. His need took him to God. Imagine how different our lives would be if we went running to God instead of running our mouth.

God's solution sounded strange to Moses: "Hit the rock."(Exodus 17:6) Hit the rock…with a stick? Was this the first baseball game? No, that was back in Genesis 1:1, in the big-inning. All jokes aside, hitting the rock was no game to Moses. I'm sure it sounded as strange to him as it does to you. Yet, Moses had learned to simply obey God's instructions. Moses wacked the rock with his rod, and life-sustaining water gushed out. It answered their real question, "Is the Lord among us or not?" (Exodus 17: 7)

It was a question that each generation continues to ask. It is a question that God answered with the gift of His Son, Emanuel, which means God with us. God's Son was sent to deliver us from the ravages of sin. He came to deliver us from fear, sickness, and eternal separation from God.[21]

This supernatural event was a paint brush in the hand of God that He used to paint a clue on the pages of Scripture to help people

---

[20]Exodus 17:1-7
[21] Isaiah 53:5

Presence - Water

unlock the mystery of redemption. Just like the rock was smitten by Moses, Jesus was smitten and crucified to redeem us from sin. "...and all of them drank the same miraculous water. For they all drank from the miraculous rock that traveled with them, and that rock was Christ." (1 Corinthians 10:4) Are you thirsty? I hope you are. Drink freely of God's refreshing, living water that was lavishly provided at the cross. Jesus, the sacrificial lamb at Calvary, completed the picture found in Exodus 17.

A second clue, related though different from the first, is tucked within the event of Numbers 20. The Israelites, again, were desperate for water. And, again, God had a solution, complete with a hidden picture. God was deliberately painting a second, connected-but-different water color picture inside His miraculous provision. He hid it for New Testament believers to uncover. God's strategy would both meet their present need and reveal His power and nature.

God told Moses to speak to the rock and promised water would flow out. The focus was on something larger than receiving water. The focus was redirected from following a powerful, committed leader to experiencing God. Though unseen, He was more real than anything their senses could experience.

Moses exploded on the people ("must we fetch you water") as if his human muscles could carry the weight of a bucket large enough or a miracle big enough to supply their need. Instead of speaking to the rock, Moses struck the rock twice, and water gushed out. The miracle was not resident in a skillful, repetitious act. The miracle was and continues to be found in Him. Miracles flow out of His presence and in obedience to His voice. This fact is emphasized by God's reprimand, "...you did not magnify my name before the people."

While I probably would have done much worse than Moses, his heated frustration and incorrect focus set in motion a single, explosive act of disobedience that had dire consequences. God's mercy released the miraculous flow of water in spite of Moses' sin.

Bringing His presence to humanity is the objective of Pentecost. No longer would God just visit mankind, but He would pack up all that He is and move inside us. We are made containers for Holy Spirit to

Pentecost Lost

inhabit by the cleansing and regenerative work of Jesus on the cross. He comes not as a demanding guest, but with gifts that move us from enjoying a well to becoming a conduit for a river. The focus is not on our talents or abilities, but it's on Him. To restate and illustrate, we should no longer be an empty clay pot. Because of Pentecost, we can have the glory of God radiating from us like a luxurious and fragrant flower growing in a pot.

This miracle happened at Kadesh, which means holiness.[22] As the revealed Word flows to and through us, we are enabled to live holy lives that bring glory to God. It takes Holy Spirit to reveal truth to us.

> I will show how holy my great name is -- the name you dishonored among the nations. And when I reveal my holiness through you before their very eyes, says the Sovereign LORD, then the nations will know that I am the LORD. [24]For I will gather you up from all the nations and bring you home again to your land. [25]Then I will sprinkle clean water on you, and you will be clean. Your filth will be washed away, and you will no longer worship idols. [26]And I will give you a new heart with new and right desires, and I will put a new spirit in you. I will take out your stony heart of sin and give you a new, obedient heart. [27]And I will put my Spirit in you so you will obey my laws and do whatever I command.
>
> ---Ezekiel 36:23-27

God said, "Speak to the rock." That would take some serious faith to walk over to the rock and talk to it in front of an angry, desperate crowd, with everyone listening. Believers today seem to face a similar dilemma. They want Holy Spirit, but they don't want to speak with tongues. Others weakly excuse their lack with, "If God wants to give me Holy Spirit, then He can." The Bible is clear. We must ask in faith to receive Holy Spirit. "If you sinful people know how to give good

---

[22]Roswell D. Hitchcock, *Hitchcock's Dictionary of Bible Names*, 1869.
http://www.biblestudytools.com/dictionaries/hitchcocks-bible-names/kadesh.html (accessed June 1, 2011)

gifts to your children, how much more will your heavenly Father give the Holy Spirit to those who ask Him?" (Luke 11:13) The focus is not the miracle of receiving His gift or the miracle of the evidence of tongues. The focus is Jesus.

Remember, this event is just a hint, not a snapshot, of what would happen at Pentecost. The picture should have been Moses speaking to the rock and water flowing out. But Moses didn't speak to it. At Pentecost, unlike Moses, the believers spoke what they were given. "And everyone present was filled with the Holy Spirit and began speaking in other languages, as the Holy Spirit gave them this ability." (Acts 2:4) God did not bypass their will to control them as if they were puppets on a string. The believers in the upper room spoke with tongues as the Spirit gave them the words, just as God was giving Moses instructions on what to say. I'm not trying to infer that Moses spoke in a language He didn't know, but I insist it was the same activity of faith that a believer must participate in to speak in tongues. Moses wanted to do what He could do in the natural. He was comfortable whacking a rock, not talking to one. God clearly reprimanded Moses for his unbelief. Often, that is what keeps believers from speaking in tongues. They want to say their words. They want to do what makes them feel comfortable instead of stepping out in faith and speaking the words they feel Holy Spirit is giving them to say.

Every believer can receive Holy Spirit. The experience will vary from person to person, but biblical evidence suggests that one thing will happen when you are filled with Holy Spirit: He will give you brand new words to speak. In Acts 2:4, the Bible says all of them began to speak. Holy Spirit did not speak. Look at the verse again-- they spoke. They partnered with Holy Spirit and spoke the words He gave them. Most of the time, Holy Spirit will speak to your spirit with thoughts. These words will come up out of your spirit and bubble up like the gurgle of a small water fountain on the wall at school. Then, as you continue to yield to Holy Spirit and speak, more words will flow out of you. As you continue to use your prayer language, you will discover the life of God changing you and empowering you to witness. This experience is more than a feeling. It is an activity as real as sap rising in a tree in spring. Holy Spirit infilling will bring spiritual growth in you like the sap promotes growth in a tree.

Speaking in tongues is not gibberish; it is a language. Holy Spirit is not a language, but when He fills believers, He gives them a prayer language to help them connect with heaven. It is not a language learned from a textbook, but it is a language that ties you to your family - your heavenly Father and Big Brother.

Alaska became the 49th state in 1959. The panoramas of Alaska are breathtaking and the wild life both menacing and captivating. The native Alaskan's ability to thrive in a land of harsh contrast and extremes is inspiring. When I visited Alaska, I wanted to learn all I could about these amazing people. One particular story was riveting.

The US government established schools in Alaska to educate their new, young citizens. Their noble goal to educate and Americanize the children took an unexpected twist. They forced the children to speak English and relegated the proliferation of their native language to home and family. The children were harshly punished if they spoke anything except English at school. Many of these schools were boarding schools. The unintended consequences of this requirement produced children who could not speak or understand their native language.

Why is the ability to speak their native language so important? It's because language ties you to your identity. It ties you to your history, your culture, and your people.

Speaking in tongues is a supernatural sign that reminds you of your heritage and connects you with your family. You are not a citizen here. You are only passing through this life. Your citizenship is in heaven. Your native language reminds you of and connects you with heaven.

Did you notice, Acts 2:4 says "began"? The beginning is only the beginning. This initial experience of speaking in tongues is only the beginning of speaking and experiencing what God has for you.

The Gateway Arch in St. Louis is a 630 foot monument that marks the place where Louis and Clark began their trek to discover and map the West. There could not have been an event to mark if Lewis and Clark had not continued from their beginning point to explore and chart the vast wilderness that lay beyond that point. When you receive the gift of Holy Spirit, this new experience is the gateway to discovering Jesus. It is the gateway or beginning point of discovering a new dimension God has for you. Some people fail to enjoy and benefit from this new adventure with God because they fail to understand it is a deepening of relationship instead of a one-time experience.

Too many people have misunderstood the infilling of Holy Spirit. He is not a one-time event that you visit so you can say "been there, done that, bought the T-shirt, worn it, and used it as a cleaning rag." When we confine the infilling of Holy Spirit to our little church-stuff or revival-once-a-year boundaries, we stay powerless, thirsty, and malnourished, continually struggling with sin and carnality. Holy Spirit infilling is the beginning of a deeper relationship, much like the marriage union deepens the relationship. When a couple gets married, they don't kiss at the front door of the church and then each go separate ways with a smile and a parting wish to "Have a nice life." No, they move into the same house. Their relationship takes on a deeper, sweeter, better, and more fulfilling dimension.

You can visit a waterfall, enjoy its beauty, hear the roar of the falls, feel the cool water spray on your face, and return home with a snapshot to share and a nice memory to retell. When you tap into the energy of that waterfall via waterwheel or power plant, it becomes more than an event. It provides sustenance when you dig a channel to your house and allow it to be your water source. It irrigates your crops and waters your livestock. Praying in tongues is a way to access God's bountiful supply. Just like any other prayer, its purpose is to worship and talk with God. Like other prayers, you should expect to receive from God. Praying in tongues builds you up. It energizes you.

A Well or a River

"But the water I give them takes away thirst altogether. It becomes a perpetual spring within them, giving them eternal life." (John 4:14) I love the reality of this truth that Jesus unveiled for the Samaritan woman. He would be an artesian well that would be in us - refreshing, renewing, and invigorating.

Pioneer families understood the importance of having their own well. They watered their livestock and quenched their thirst from the waters of their well. But Jesus expands His discourse from a personal well to a vast river. "On the last day, the climax of the festival, Jesus stood and shouted to the crowds, '...If you are thirsty, come to me!'" (John 7:37*)* This reference points to the Feast of Tabernacles, the last of the three mandatory feasts.

As the Israelites traveled through the wilderness, they lived in tents that could be carried as they moved from place to place. These temporary homes were called tabernacles. God did not want them to forget those years in the wilderness, so one more feast, the Feast of Tabernacles, was added to the Jewish calendar. This feast required them to build and stay in a tent or a simple lean-to structure made of branches and tree limbs until the end of the feast. God's intent was greater than reiterating a historical event. It was more than a motivational reminder of triumph over difficult circumstances. This feast was a reminder of His Presence during those difficult times. (He had provided for their every need. Sweet manna lay on the ground like tiny frosted flakes.) The Feast of Tabernacles celebrated the presence of Almighty God that accompanied them in the wilderness. Every day, they were guided by a cloud, and at night, a pillar of fire warmed them. They enjoyed all these benefits because God was present with them. This feast celebrated His presence and His provision. Samuel Chadwick states:

> There are few incidents more illuminating than that recorded of "the last day of the Feast," in John 7:37-39. The Feast was the Feast of Tabernacles. The Feast proper lasted seven days, during which all Israel dwelt in booths. Special sacrifices were offered and special rites observed. Every morning one of the priests brought water from the pool of Siloam, and amidst the sounding of trumpets and other demonstrations of joy the water was poured upon the altar. The rite was a celebration and a prophecy. It commemorated the miraculous supply of water in the wilderness, and it bore witness to the expectation of the coming of the Spirit. On the

seventh day the ceremony of the poured water ceased, but the eighth day was a day of holy convocation, the greatest day of all. On that day there was no water poured upon the altar, and it was on the waterless day that Jesus stood on the spot and cried, saying: "If any man thirst, let him come unto Me and drink." Then He added these words: "He that believeth on Me, as the Scripture hath said, from within him shall flow rivers of living water." The Apostle adds the interpretive comment: "But this spake He of the Spirit, which they that believe on Him were to receive: for the Spirit was not yet given; because Jesus was not yet glorified."[23]

The well is for personal benefit, but the scope and influence of a river far surpasses a well. Your salvation is a personal thing, like a well. The river never belonged to the homestead. The river gushed and gurgled in and through, coursing out and on to others. A well blesses a family, but a river blesses everyone wherever it goes. That is the purpose of the infilling of precious Holy Spirit: to flow out of your life to bless others everywhere you go.

Are you dry? Begin to speak to the rock, Jesus. Ask Him to fill you with precious Holy Spirit. He is the one who baptizes with Holy Spirit. Focus on Jesus, just as if He were standing in the room with you. Don't get distracted by what is going on around you. Believe that He wants to and will fill you. From deep within your spirit, begin to worship Jesus aloud. Express to Jesus how much you love Him. Listen to your spirit, but focus on Jesus. Holy Spirit will give you the words to speak. You may only hear a single syllable but speak the sound He gives you. Don't copy someone else. Words may bubble up from your spirit. Or, perhaps you may feel like your tongue wants to say things different than the words you are trying to form. Don't try to stop it. A word or syllable may keep coming up in your mind; speak it out. Holy Spirit supplies the words. You simply speak out what He gives you. Relax. Don't think about speaking a new

---

[23] Samuel Chadwick, *The Way to Pentecost*,
http://www.raptureready.com/resource/chadwick/chadwick32.html
(accessed June 1, 2011)

language. Focus on Jesus. You may feel silly but keep speaking what you have been given. As you obey Him, you will receive more words.

If you want to play first baseman on your ball team, you move beside first base and position yourself to catch the ball. You wouldn't stand out in left field. If you want to receive precious Holy Spirit, you must position yourself to receive Him. Praise and worship positions you to receive Holy Spirit. Your worship is an invitation for God to come near.

Our emphasis at kid's camp one year was to receive and know precious Holy Spirit. The mom of one of the girls came as a counselor and was hoping to receive Holy Spirit herself. At the end of the service, children filled the altar to experience the powerful presence of God. As if on cue, the counselors moved around the children praying at the altar and engaged almost simultaneously. Several children began to speak in tongues, while others were weeping and worshipping on the floor. I spotted this mom and, without knowing her story, I recognized God wanted to fill her. I encouraged her to open her mouth and begin to speak. I said, "That's Holy Spirit. Speak it out."

I had never seen anything like it before. When she began to speak, it was like opening a fire hydrant. Her new language gushed out. It was powerful. Still, other people are filled with equal supernatural power without experiencing such a spectacular feeling. Be careful that you do not allow the expectation of an emotional experience to rob you of experiencing the supernatural infilling of Holy Spirit. Spectacular feeling and supernatural infilling is not the same thing.

Keep the rivers flowing in your life by continuing to pray in tongues. Pray in the Spirit every day! Join the Apostle Paul in praying with your understanding and praying in the Spirit. Praying in the Spirit is praying with your prayer language. When you pray in the Spirit, you may not understand the words, but God understands what you are saying. It is like having a shortcut on your computer desktop. It takes you directly to where you want to go. It doesn't need to be interpreted or unzipped because it is your private prayer language.

Presence - Water

Praying in your prayer language builds you up. It energizes you to overcome sin and be more effective in every area of your life.

Sinaqua

I should have known better. I should have realized that Montezuma's Castle[24] was not what it seemed to be. We were in Sedona, Arizona, to see God's handiwork, the magnificent red rock formations. After driving to the national park, we walked down a scenic, winding path, anticipating a king's castle. Instead, we saw the homes of an ancient group of cliff-dwelling Indians, built high in the crevices of the mountain, like a cliff swallow's nest. They formed walls with rocks, dabbing crevices like a mud dauber, to construct private residences. "This twenty-roomed, high-rise apartment nestled into a towering limestone cliff tells a 1,000 year-old story of ingenuity and survival in an unforgiving desert landscape."[25] Scientists named these people the Sinaqua Indians. Sinaqua means "no water." Where there's no water, there's no life.

The end of sin brings death, just as surely as being in the desert without water brings death. This fact is true, whether referring to a church, a family, or a person. If you don't have Jesus, the living water, you are spiritually dead. As believers and churches have become too busy and too self-sufficient, the life-giving waters have stopped flowing, resulting in spiritual drought.

The Sinaqua Indians found water. Maybe they found the river the same way most travelers do. Perhaps the change in terrain from barren to a lush tree line signaled the presence of water. The river that ran through the park was lined on both sides with trees, both scraggly cottonwoods and magnificent sycamores. The Sinaqua Indians, like the trees, wanted to be near the water, so they built their homes in the cliffs above the water. The high places protected them from flash floods and attacks from their enemies. Building materials were readily available.

---

[24]http://www.nps.gov/moca/historyculture/index.htm (accessed June 1, 2011)
[25] Ibid.

Pentecost Lost

Eleven miles away, another Sinaquan apartment complex was built around an amazing artesian well. It was named Montezuma's Well. The well was "formed long ago by the collapse of the roof of a limestone cavern. Over one million gallons of water a day flows continuously into the well from beneath. This constant supply of fresh water provides an aquatic habitat like no other in the world and has served as an oasis for wildlife and humans for thousands of years."[26] They built their lives around this life-sustaining well. The birds and animals that gathered there provided food for the cliff dwellers, and fresh, clean water bubbled up every day for their drinking and cooking.

But they weren't content to just drink the water. Their fields were dry. They needed water for their fields so they could feed their children. They spent long hours of back breaking labor without the aid of modern machinery to carve a canal in solid rock. Slowly, laboriously, they chiseled an irrigation canal to the fields to water their crops. More than 500 years later, the canal is still there, with fresh, crystal clear, life-giving water flowing through it. They paid the price to enjoy the benefits of water.

Jesus paid the price so we can enjoy the life-giving benefits of spiritual water. Just as there can be no life without water, we are dead spiritually without Jesus. Jesus is the only way to have eternal life hereafter and abundant life now.

In John 7, the metaphor is expanded. "If you believe in me, come and drink! For the Scriptures declare that rivers of living water will flow out from within." (John 7:38)

We know about rivers. They twist and turn, changing the topography or landscape of mountains and fields. As the water courses through cities and forests, its movement tosses and tumbles rocks until their edges are smooth. We know about rivers. We swim in them, fish in them, and hunt wildlife around them. We picnic on their banks and name songs after them. Wildlife hides in the brush and trees along its edges and drinks its life-giving water. From the

---

[26]http://www.nps.gov/moca/montezuma-well.htm (accessed June 1, 2001)

earliest times, cities and homes were built around rivers. We know about rivers, but one flowing from a believer needs some clarification.

God was giving readers a picture to help us understand what the Baptism of Holy Spirit would be like. Just as a river coursing through the land brings life, a believer brings the life of God to people. A river changes a desert into an oasis. A river brings abundant life to a desert and transforms it in almost every way. People are God's representatives in the Earth. We are His agents of change. His love should flow through us and out to people, so they can experience His love, His power, and His grace.

We should never be satisfied to experience God's abundant life alone. We should want to share Jesus with others. That effort is more effective when empowered by God's river flowing through us. There are people surrounding us who need Jesus. We can pray more effectively for our unsaved family and friends when we pray in the Spirit. We can be a more effective witness through the power of Holy Spirit, as He flows out of us to meet the needs of others. He will guide us to the right person at the right time. He will help us know what to say and how to show His love in a way that will open people's hearts.

I just have to say it one more time: Keep the river flowing by praying in tongues.

The ruins of their homes, shards of pottery, and primitive tools that have been uncovered distinguish the Sinaqua Indians from other tribes. But, there is a mystery surrounding these Indians. They seemed to have mysteriously disappeared. Scientists believe that the Sinaqua Indians must have joined other tribes of Indians, adapting and blending into their lifestyles until their distinctiveness was totally lost. It is sad to think that the Sinaqua Indians forgot who they were and lost the uniqueness that made them a special group of people.

The Baptism of Holy Spirit was a distinctive of the early church. It was a distinctive that made them both Pentecostal and powerful. They were not Pentecostal in a denominational sense. They were Pentecostal because the events of Pentecost affected their lives in every way. When we exempt Holy Spirit from our belief system, we cease to be Pentecostal. We lose more than the name. We lose the

Pentecost Lost

power that enables us to become all God intended for us. We are not favored in the sense of entitlement for special privileges. We are favored in the sense that we are a conduit as we allow His life to flow through us and out to others.

Think about it:
___

DUI: Dwell Under the Influence

Dear God, What do you want me to take away from this chapter?

Is there a barren area in my life that needs some water?

Make room for and expect Holy Spirit's life-giving presence to fill you in a deeper way.

Chapter Three

Promised - Gift

Complete Picture

There's an old tale from India about three, curious, blind men trying to describe an elephant.

The first blind man ran his hands over the elephant's belly. Confidently he described his discovery to his friends, "An elephant is like a wall."

"How ridiculous," his friend scoffed, "an elephant is like a tree," he insisted, as he ran his hand around the huge leg of the elephant.

Shaking his head, the third man could only chuckle as he clutched the elephant's tail. "You are both wrong. An elephant is like a snake. It is long and skinny," he chided.

What they could not see was that each of them was correct in their observation. With their limited ability and perspective, each described a different feature of an elephant.

Even when standing on our tip-toes, our reach can exceed our grasp. Our ability to comprehend the nature of Holy Spirit fails to scratch even a thin layer of who He is. The vastness of Holy Spirit is unfathomable. Often people discover a single attribute of His character and stop there. We see Holy Spirit brooding at creation, like a bird broods over her eggs. Still, that powerful picture is incomplete. We see Him drawing people to Christ, like a magnet, and conclude we know Him. But, He is unfathomable. He is beyond the grasp of human reasoning. In this lesson, we will move closer and linger longer to discover fresh revelation and to be rejuvenated by the experience.

Eye has not seen...but

There's a corny old riddle that reminds me of Paul's words in 1 Corinthians. What has ears but cannot hear? What has eyes but cannot see? An ear of corn cannot hear, and a potato has eyes but cannot see. I warned you that it was corny. Paul carries the metaphor farther in 1 Corinthians 2:9 with the intriguing proclamation that "no eye has seen and no ear has heard what God has prepared for people that love Him." Throughout scripture, we see a progressive unfolding of the revelation of the nature of God. "God did not reveal it to previous generations, but now he has revealed it by the Holy Spirit to his holy apostles and prophets." (Ephesians 3:5) Paul explained to the Ephesian church that past generations could not understand the mystery of Christ because God had not shown it yet.

It is hard for me to imagine that someone could fail to understand that God carefully watches over each individual. But, Hagar was shocked when she suddenly realized that God saw her.[27] The Jewish patriarch, Abraham, suddenly recognized God as his provider in Genesis 22:14. Numerous Old Testament truths were shrouded with mystery, hidden from curious eyes, so they could be revealed later, like an orange being peeled to reveal sweet fruit.

The inability to see and hear is not the illustration that should be gleaned from this passage of scripture. We stopped too quickly; let's read verse 10. "But..." (Do you know what the conjunction "but" means? It means forget everything you just read; it's all about to change. You've said it, "She's a nice person, but"...then you go on to paint an entirely different picture of her.) In 1 Corinthians 2:10, Paul said, "No eye has seen, no ear has heard, and no mind has imagined what God has prepared for those who love him. [10]But we know these things because God has revealed them to us by his Spirit, and his Spirit searches out everything and shows us even God's deep secrets." Did

---

[27] Genesis 16:13

you get that? God wants to reveal the things He has already prepared for you. He reveals things to you like your Grandma lifts the cover off your favorite dessert. Or, a more accurate comparison is the revelation that takes place on Extreme Home Makeovers when they move the bus to disclose their new creation to the astonished home owner. The homeowners are not allowed onsite until the makeover is complete, and only then are they allowed to see the finished product. Pentecost was the date on God's calendar to reveal precious Holy Spirit to the world.

> No, the wisdom we speak of is the secret wisdom of God, which was hidden in former times, though he made it for our benefit before the world began. [8]But the rulers of this world have not understood it; if they had, they would never have crucified our glorious Lord.   --1 Corinthians 2:7-8

God has divine secrets He wants to unwrap for you to understand and enjoy. Think about it. Do you realize that the Bible is the only book that you will never understand unless you know the author? Precious Holy Spirit holds the only light that brings life and revelation to the truth found within Scripture. You can know all about the Bible, memorize every word perfectly, and never unlock the treasures of truth that abound in its pages.

Google is arguably the world's largest search engine. The Google search engine is used so frequently that the verb, "google," was officially added to the Oxford English Dictionary and the Merriam-Webster Collegiate Dictionary in 2006. Yet, Holy Spirit is truly the greatest search engine. He searches not the largest hard drive but the drive of the greatest heart - God's heart - for secrets that will bless you and enlarge your ability to live a victorious and vibrant life for Jesus Christ.

"No, the wisdom we speak of is the secret wisdom of God, which was hidden in former times, though he made it for our benefit before the world began." (1 Corinthians 2:7) God hasn't hidden things from us like a child who has hidden a favorite candy bar from his or her candy-snitching sibling. God has hidden gold and diamonds in the ground, so we will appreciate their value. Similarly, God has hidden nuggets of truth to increase their perceived value. We experience a deeper level of relationship with God as He guides us on our search, like a parent guiding a child hunting Easter eggs. According to 1 Corinthians 2:7, God's secrets are for our glory and benefit, so He will be glorified in our life.

Pentecost is one of those precious treasures that God hid for believers to find. He hid secrets about Holy Spirit in a time capsule with a date stamp to be opened at Pentecost. This revelation opened the door for believers to receive the fullness of Holy Spirit, so we could reflect His glory, magnificence, and grandeur. But, somehow, that revelation of Pentecost has become buried under layers of skepticism, fear, and ignorance.

The Promise

"You promise?" You've heard it and said it, especially as a child. We want to verify the purposefulness of someone's words with the guarantee of a promise. There are all kinds of promises: 1. Exaggerated promises from a manufacturer that its product will produce astonishing results, 2. Manipulative promises, not unlike those of children, "I'll be your best friend, if you…,"3. Good intention promises, "I'll give you a call next week", but without follow through, and 4. Empty promises or outright lies, without any fulfillment intentions, are the most difficult to understand. For varied reasons, the declaration that a person or a product will do something often far exceeds the follow through or the fulfillment of that promise. A promise causes us to look to the future with a hope of something better. Confidence in a promise propels us to action. It causes us to work harder, to purchase a product, or to marry someone. Hope is tied to a promise, which is tied to the integrity of the person or company that issues the promise. A promise is only as solid as the entity behind the promise.

God gave Abram a promise in Genesis 15:13-14, 18

Promised-Gift

Then the LORD told Abram, You can be sure that your descendants will be strangers in a foreign land, and they will be oppressed as slaves for four hundred years. ^{14}But I will punish the nation that enslaves them, and in the end they will come away with great wealth.^{18}He promised: "Yes, I will give all this land of Canaan to you and to your offspring forever. And I will be their God."

Joseph was so confident that God would keep His promise that he made his descents promise to take his bones with them when they left for the Promised Land. God didn't forget His promise; He delivered the Jewish people supernaturally. Forty more years passed, one year for every day the spies checked out the land of Canaan. Everyone older than forty at the time of the rebellion, including Moses and Aaron, excluding Joshua and Caleb, were dead. Still, God's promise remained alive. A new generation stood at the brink of the flooding Jordan River, at the edge of the fulfillment of God's Promise. When they crossed this river, they would be in the land God promised to them hundreds of years prior. The Promised Land was not a picture of heaven. There were no battles to be won in heaven. Rather, it was a picture of the blessed life that God wanted them to enjoy.

The Jordan River was an agent of stark and drastic change as it cut its way through the desert terrain. It was also a symbol of the change that was about to take place as the Israelites stood on its banks. Things would never be the same for them. First, their nomadic travels would stop, and they would take up permanent residency in the land God had promised. Second, the manna was going to stop, so they would need to take food with them (Joshua 1:11). And, third, there would be no cloud or fire to guide them. [28]

God had two specific instructions to move them into position to receive the promise: First, cleanse yourself. Second, follow the ark.

Let's look at Joshua 3:2-4:

"Three days later, the Israelite leaders went through the camp ^{3}giving these instructions to the people: "When you see

---

[28] Joshua 1- 3

the Levitical priests carrying the Ark of the Covenant of the LORD your God, follow them. ⁴Since you have never traveled this way before, they will guide you. Stay about a half mile behind them, keeping a clear distance between you and the Ark. Make sure you don't come any closer."

What is the significance of following the Ark of the Covenant? This golden ark carried on the shoulders of the priests held the commandments of God, Aaron's rod that budded, and a jar of manna. The lid of the ark was the mercy seat, a symbol of the presence of God. They were instructed to follow the ark because they didn't know the route to get where they needed to go. "Then Joshua told the people, 'Purify yourselves, for tomorrow the LORD will do great wonders among you.'" (Joshua 3:5) They would see the miraculous, supernatural hand of God in demonstration. When the priests stepped into the water with the Ark, the waters dried up and the people crossed the Jordan River on dry ground. God was revealing His presence through a supernatural miracle. They saw the Ark and the miracle, but they failed to see the truth hidden in this event. In order to enjoy the fulfillment of the promise, they had to follow the Word of God and the Spirit of God.

Joshua's command to the Israelites should echo through the ages to touch the ears of the modern Church. "Follow the ark. You haven't been this way before." The things that worked in the past don't work anymore. Follow the ark. Following the ark means obeying biblical principles and guidelines. It includes submission to spiritual authority and receiving supernatural provision. The New Testament Church embraces and expands the principles and benefits embodied in the imagery of the magnificent Ark of the Covenant. Let me explain by taking you back to the Jordan River.

Let's fast forward from that time through the pages of scripture to another miraculous event at the River Jordan. John, the cousin of Jesus, was baptizing believers. Jesus approached John with a request to be baptized. John was totally bewildered; why would Jesus, the Son of God, ask to be baptized? Jesus insisted that baptism was a significant act of obedience. In response to His request, John and Jesus waded into the murky waters of the Jordan River. Through the eyes of scripture, we see two men in the water; one was the perfect Son of God. Standing there in the Jordan River, Jesus was submitting to the plan of His Father. However, this ordinary baptism took on extraordinary significance when Holy Spirit descended and rested on Jesus in the form of a dove.

Again, the Jordan River was a symbol of radical change; Jesus was about to institute a New Covenant. Jesus, the living Word, was about to establish a covenant of grace, where sin would be eradicated instead of covered. The death of Christ on the Cross would supernaturally rip the veil from top to bottom that separated us from the presence of God. Because of Jesus, we have access into His presence. The picture conveyed through water baptism is an illustration that believers are dead to their old life and to sin. A new, clean, vibrant creation is symbolized as they come up out of the water. Baptism is an important act of obedience. If you have not been baptized in water, I encourage you to do so.

The significance of this event does not end with the act of water baptism. Holy Spirit descended on Jesus in the form of a dove, empowering Him to do the works of the Father. "Then Jesus, full of the Holy Spirit, left the Jordan River. He was led by the Spirit to go out into the wilderness." (Luke 4:1)"Then Jesus returned to Galilee, filled with the Holy Spirit's power. Soon he became well known throughout the surrounding country."(Luke 4.14) It was out of this experience through Holy Spirit that His miracles flowed. These people were about to see what The Promise fulfilled would look like. Jesus modeled for us a Spirit-filled life. Jack Hayford says:

> Jesus is the prototype of the Spirit-filled, Spirit-empowered life. The Book of Acts is the story of the disciples receiving what Jesus received in order to do what Jesus did.[29]

---

[29] Jack Hayford, *Hayford's Bible Handbook*, (© 1995,Thomas Nelson, Inc.) 326.

Pentecost Lost

That's why He could assure His followers in John 14:12 that they would do greater works. He understood the magnitude of the promise of the Father. The fulfillment of that promise - the arrival of Holy Spirit - would enable believers to do and be like Christ. Holy Spirit baptism is the gateway to the signs and wonders they saw Jesus perform. God could have chosen a different route for the miracles to flow; however, out of His Sovereignty, He chose this one.

God knew His people needed more than a new location. God's vision for His people as outlined in Exodus 19 was for them each to be kings and priest, effecting change everywhere they went, but their human efforts failed. God spoke His laws to them audibly, powerfully, dramatically, and supernaturally in Exodus 20. He wrote them on stone tablets, and they were kept in the precious, golden Ark under the Mercy Seat. But rules weren't enough. God's answer was to move from external rules to internal change and support: "And I will give them singleness of heart and put a new spirit within them. I will take away their hearts of stone and give them tender hearts instead..." (Ezekiel 11:19) That reality is reemphasized in the New Testament: "This is the new covenant I will make with my people on that day, says the Lord: I will put my laws in their hearts so they will understand them, and I will write them on their minds so they will obey them." (Hebrews 10:16) This is an inner work of Holy Spirit.

The coming of precious Holy Spirit on the day of Pentecost was the fulfillment of a greater promise than that held by the Jewish people of possessing a bountiful land. The Promise was the person of Holy Spirit, the empowering presence of Almighty God. "Through the work of Christ Jesus, God has blessed the Gentiles with the same blessing he promised to Abraham, and we Christians receive the promised Holy Spirit through faith." (Galatians 3:14) The heart change, which came through the redemptive work of Christ, produced a desire within us to please God because we love Him. Subsequently, the indwelling presence of Holy Spirit enables us to follow through. The focus of our actions is changed from good activities to relational overflow. "He did this so that the requirement of the law would be fully accomplished for us who no longer follow our sinful nature but instead follow the Spirit." (Romans 8:4) "...that I will pour out my spirit..." (Acts 2:17b)

Promised-Gift

Precious Holy Spirit is not another promise, nor one of many, but He is the fulfillment of the Promise of the Father.

William Robinson Clark writes:

> It was, in a certain sense, an answer to the prayers of the disciples; but it was also the fulfillment of the Divine promise. It was the work of God, and this thought is made more emphatic by the addition of the words, "from heaven." The gift came down from God out of heaven; nay, rather, it was God and heaven coming down to dwell with man on the earth.[30]

Samuel Chadwick states:

> The Divine Spirit is called "Holy Spirit of Promise." The expression looks both backward and forward. He is the Spirit given in fulfillment of promise, and in Him is the earnest of the promise as yet unfulfilled. The gift of Pentecost fulfills the crowning promise of the Father. The Spirit is the Promised One. Our Lord spoke of Him as "the promise of the Father," and on the day of Pentecost the Apostle Peter, in explanation of the descent of Holy Spirit, declared: "This Jesus did God raise up, whereof we all are witnesses. Being therefore by the right hand of God exalted, and having received of the Father the promise of the Holy Ghost, He hath poured forth this, which we see and hear." Pentecost was God's seal upon the Messiah-ship of Jesus, and the fulfilling of His promise to Israel. Fulfillment brings new promises. Attainment inspires new hopes.[31]

"But our High Priest has been given a ministry that is far superior to the ministry of those who serve under the old laws, for he is the one who guarantees for us a better covenant with God, based on better promises." (Hebrews 8:6) "This new covenant is based on better promises: He is the one who has enabled us to represent his new covenant. This is a covenant, not of written laws, but of the Spirit. The

---

[30] Clark, *The Paraclete*, 106.
[31] Chadwick, *The Way to Pentecost*, 10, *http://wesley.nnu.edu/wesleyctr/books/0401-0500/HDM0496.pdf*

old way ends in death; in the new way, the Holy Spirit gives life. ⁷That old system of law etched in stone led to death, yet it began with such glory that the people of Israel could not bear to look at Moses' face. For his face shone with the glory of God, even though the brightness was already fading away. ⁸Shouldn't we expect far greater glory when the Holy Spirit is giving life?" (2 Corinthians 3:6-8)

The Spirit gives life. The Spirit of the New Covenant would be more glorious, more wonderful, and more miraculous than the previous covenant. Holy Spirit is God's active, energizing agent in the hearts of believers today.

Since July 2010, American homemakers have discovered dirty dishes in the dishwashers after running a complete dishwashing cycle. The problem is not broken or defective dishwashers but a change in environmental laws. SLS or phosphate, a highly effective active agent in detergents, was removed from laundry detergents in 1993, but dishwashing detergents were exempted from the law. On July 1, 2010, sixteen states enacted laws to limit the levels of phosphates in dishwashing detergent to no more than .5%. Without sufficient amounts of the active agent, SLS, the new formula of most dishwashing detergents leaves a white film on dishes. This has prompted many consumers to wrongly suspect a defective washing machine and call a repairman. Many consumers have had to replace dishes, which were damaged by the new detergent.[32]

Too many believers have failed to embrace the active agent, precious Holy Spirit, in their lives. As a result, they arduously look for a solution that will enable them to live a victorious Christian life. "They will act religious, but they will reject the power that could make them godly. Stay away from people like that!" (2 Timothy 3:5) God's formula for life doesn't work when we exempt the active agent, Holy Spirit.

---

[32] Fox News January 25, 2011, Why Aren't Your Dishes Getting Clean? New Environmental Laws by Scott Iskowitz;
http://www.foxnews.com/scitech/2011/01/25/arent-dishes-getting-clean-new-environmental-laws/ (accessed June 1, 2011)

For Me?

Do you remember how you felt when your teacher began her mental process to select a student to do something special? Did you wave your hand and call out, "Pick me. Pick me!"?

Then, when the teacher pointed at you, you looked around and asked, "Me?" Nodding her head, the teacher continued, "Yes, you!"

That seems to be the question the modern church continues to ask regarding the infilling of Holy Spirit, "Me? It's for me?" Let's settle that question by reading a quote from an Old Testament prophet that Peter referred to on the day of Pentecost. It is found in Joel 2:28a: "Then, after doing all those things, I will pour out my Spirit upon all people." Peter presented the initial descent of the Spirit on the Day of Pentecost as a mighty inauguration of the last days, in which all of God's people will be baptized, or filled, with the Spirit (Acts 2:17,18). Who will God's Spirit be poured upon? Now look closely. What did that verse say? All people! Is there any possible way we could be confused and not know upon whom God would pour out His Spirit?

Let's look at the complete verses in Joel 2:28, 29:

> Then after I have poured out my rains again, I will pour out my Spirit upon all people. Your sons and daughters will prophesy. Your old men will dream dreams. Your young men will see visions. ²⁹In those days, I will pour out my Spirit even on servants, men and women alike.

I am so thankful that sons, daughters, old men, young men, and servants were all included. But the recipient list didn't stop with Peter's generation. Acts 2:39 reads: "The promise is to you, and to your children, and even to the Gentiles - all who have been called by the Lord our God." Yes, the Promised Present is for you!

While the thought of a wonderful gift and a significant promise should excite and engage us, many believers remain reticent and suspicious, in much the same way they would refuse a free gift offer from an obvious shyster. Ignorant of its intrinsic value and abundant benefits, we are reluctant to receive His gift; or, our cocky self-confidence blinds our ability to perceive our need for an added gift.

Our modern church culture doesn't seem to know very much about precious Holy Spirit. He seems to have been banished to the basement or some back room, along with all the weird, flaky, fringe elements, and is treated with the same skepticism as one might treat the notion of a spooky ghost. Precious Holy Spirit is just as real and just as much God as Jesus the Son or God the Father. Let's remove the shroud of mysticism, and talk about Him. First, Holy Spirit is not an "it" or a thing. He is a person with a distinct personality. He has feelings and can be grieved. "And do not grieve Holy Spirit of God, with whom you were sealed for the day of redemption." (Ephesians 4:30 NIV) He has a mind. "And the Father who knows all hearts knows what the Spirit is saying, for the Spirit pleads for us believers in harmony with God's own will." (Romans 8:27) It is through Him that we have access to the Father. "Now all of us, both Jews and Gentiles, may come to the Father through the same Holy Spirit because of what Christ has done for us." (Ephesians 2:18)

The Good Gift

The American culture celebrates by giving and receiving gifts. Birthdays, anniversaries, and holidays, especially Christmas, are celebrated with gifts.

Occasionally, hopefully not too often, we have received a bad gift; one so bad that we can't wait to get rid of it. Sometimes we re-gift, or give the gift to someone else, hoping they'll like it better than we did. The key to successful re-gifting is remembering from whom you received the gift, so you don't give it back to the original gift giver.

Most gifts are good, and some gifts go way beyond good. Some gifts go all the way to "GREAT" on the gift gauge. When searching for a special gift for that extraordinary person in our life, we often tell the sales clerk we are looking for "the perfect gift." It must be the right size. It must fit the personality of the person receiving the gift. It must

Promised-Gift

be something they would enjoy. It must convey the love and significance behind the gift. It must be both beautiful and of quality construction. What would move a gift into the perfect gift category for you?

God's perfect gift is exactly what you need, more than you can imagine. His extravagant love and inexhaustible bounty are reflected in the Perfect Gift that was unwrapped at Pentecost. It is an amazing, wonderful, absolutely brilliant gift that He has chosen to give to you. Holy Spirit is God's perfect Gift.

Luke 11 douses the fear that God's gift will be something bad. He asks the question with a prefaced qualifier: you are imperfect. In spite of your imperfections, if your hungry children beg you for a piece of bread, are you going to give them a rock to gnaw on? Or if they ask you for a piece of meat are you going to toss them a live venomous snake? The implied answer is no. We love our kids, and we want what is best for them.[33] We work hard to provide good things and to lavish them with gifts to enjoy.

Building on that foundation that even evil people want to lavish their children with good things, God explains His gift is good, really good. "If you sinful people know how to give good gifts to your children, how much more will your heavenly Father give the Holy Spirit to those who ask him." (Luke 11:13) God's gift is not an ominous gift to approach timorously. Our culture, or more aptly satan, has cloaked this gift in lies. You can trust the goodness of your heavenly Father that would never give you something bad.

I wish I had vocabulary to help you understand how wonderful the Gift of Holy Spirit really is. Or, that I could paint a picture that would help you see His beautiful nature. I would love to give you a taste or take your hand and help you touch the reality of His presence, but I cannot do any of those things. You must do that yourself. Sincerely and deeply, open yourself to taste and see that the Lord is good. I can only point you in the right direction. I can only tell you how precious He is to me, and share my experiences with you.

---

[33] Luke 11:11-12 author's wording

Pentecost Lost

You will never really understand until you step out in faith to experience the dazzling wonders of His presence and power flowing through you.

When I Received

I was young, but I still remember my first visit to a church that believed in the baptism of the Holy Spirit. People were jammed and crammed into the front of the church, with their hands jabbed in the air, speaking funny-sounding words. I had never been in a service like that.

When I was twelve years old, my friend, Alicia, invited me to church. Reluctantly, my mom agreed. She warned me that Alicia's church was a little different, but nothing had prepared me for the drastic difference I observed. I stretched my neck to search the faces of the people to see if they were in pain or if they were as frightened as I was. Instead of seeing fear or anguish, their faces were radiant, almost as if a light bulb was behind them. Their smiles were the biggest I had ever seen, even though I could see tears tracking down their cheeks.

I had so many questions. Alicia's mom tried to explain what was happening, "When people really love Jesus, they somehow run out of words to explain how much they love Him. God gives us a new language to help us express our love to Him. We may not understand the words, but God does, and He receives their sincere expression of love and thankfulness. These people are excited because they love Jesus. There's nothing to be afraid of, Sweetheart."

While I didn't understand everything the lady told me, I wasn't afraid anymore. I had lots of questions. As soon as we settled in the car, I began my barrage of questions. How did those people get their new language? Can anybody get a new language? Can little kids get that new language?

Alicia's parents answered as patiently and thoroughly as they knew how. "God has a very special gift He wants to give all His children. That gift is the infilling of Holy Spirit."

Promised-Gift

"What is the infilling of Holy Spirit," I questioned. "I thought we were talking about those people talking in a funny language."

Alicia's mom explained, "When a person receives Holy Spirit, they speak with a new language. Anyone who has received Jesus as Savior can receive Holy Spirit."

I was completely amazed that even little kids could be filled with Holy Spirit. Excited, I hurried home and told my Mom everything I had learned.

"I," my Mother calmly began, "I don't want you going to that church anymore. We have our own church, and I don't want you going there again."

"But Mother, we only go Sunday mornings. Can't I go with Alicia on Sunday nights?" I protested.

The answer was still no. I was so disappointed. I wanted to go to Alicia's church. I wanted to be filled with Holy Spirit, but now I couldn't. Or could I? Oh, I would never sneak behind my mother's back, but God could change my mother's mind. I began to ask God to let me go to Alicia's church. I prayed every time I thought about church, which was pretty often.

Sunday afternoon, I finally got the nerve to talk to my mom about going to church with Alicia. "Mother, can I go to church with Alicia tonight?" The silence seemed like an eternity, as I prayed under my breath.

"Oh, I don't mind if you go tonight," Mother finally answered.

I was so excited, "I'll call Alicia and tell her I can go!"

That night, I listened carefully to every word the minister spoke. I knew I was there only because God had answered my prayer. If He would answer that prayer, maybe He would answer my prayer to be filled with Holy Spirit.

As the people gathered at the front of the church, I joined them, expecting to receive God's precious gift. I lifted my hands and began telling Jesus how much I loved Him. Alicia's mom laid her hand gently on my shoulder and quietly began praying in what she called her "prayer language."

Pentecost Lost

I closed my eyes and worshipped Jesus. As I worshipped, I realized I was saying something that sounded funny. The words sounded funny to my ears, but I knew this must be my new language. I continued to allow the words to bubble from my mouth as the joy bubbled in my heart. I had never felt anything like this. I felt a love for people that I had never felt. I felt so happy. I wanted to tell everyone what had happened to me.

The Gift of Language

Language is a powerful gift that enables us to communicate. We crossed the border into Mexico to shop in Tijuana. I only knew one word in Spanish "baño," which means bathroom. My heavy southern accent shaped the word into a sound that was hardly recognizable by the store attendant. But, I finally communicated sufficiently to be escorted to the little comfort station in the back of the store. I am sure we would all agree that it is beneficial to learn the language before you visit a country that speaks a different language. No one gets upset when they hear someone speak French or Spanish. No one is offended when Chinese tourists converse in Chinese. You may not understand the language. You may be curious or wish you understood what they were saying, but you won't be upset that they were speaking a different language.

Yet, so many people miss what God has for them because they do not want to speak with tongues. Some people have been taught that tongues are from the devil. Others have been taught that tongues have passed away.

When you understand a language, you can communicate thoughts, feelings, and strategies effectively. But, do you realize you can benefit from a language, even if you don't understand it?

Computer language is a total mystery to me, yet I benefit from it every day. The computer has become my lifeline for knowledge, efficiency, and networking. Computer programs for a windows-based computer will not work on a different operating system. My website is written with a program that allows me to produce a website using templates without knowing a single html script. I can select a view that allows me to see the scripts that cause my webpage to function properly, but I don't understand it. The software writes the computer language for me. The software does what I cannot do.

I don't read computer language. I don't write computer language. I don't understand computer language. But I benefit from it every single day of my life! Why? I benefit because I use my computer every day. I use it even though I don't understand it. Yet, so many sincerely hungry believers come to a complete stop in their walk with God because they do not understand tongues. I've heard people say, "I want Holy Spirit, but I don't want tongues." That's like saying I want the front side of a dime, but I don't want the back side of it. Or, it is like saying I want an oak tree, but I don't want leaves.

The heavenly language you receive the moment you yield to Holy Spirit is an amazing gift. It is different than the gift of tongues, which is a sign for the unbeliever. It is a wonderful, powerful language that allows you to bypass your mind and emotions in order to pray more effectively than you can even realize. It is a language requiring a partnership. Precious Holy Spirit provides the words, and you provide the voice. You yield your will and voice to pray the perfect will of God. "And the Father who knows all hearts knows what the Spirit is saying, for the Spirit pleads for us believers in harmony with God's own will." (Romans 8:27) It is not gibberish. It is a Holy Spirit-inspired prayer. "For anyone who speaks in a tongue does not speak to men but to God. Indeed, no one understands him; he utters mysteries with his spirit." (1 Corinthians 14:2 NIV) When you pray in the Spirit, or tongues, you are praying divine strategy. You are praying about things that God wants you to pray about.

Have you ever downloaded pictures or a large program online that had to be zipped or compressed before it could be downloaded? Well, that is exactly what God does in your spirit. Often, as you pray regularly in the Spirit, God will download amazing spiritual truths and understanding into your spirit. The Apostle Paul had such amazing revelation from God. He wrote most of the New Testament. Paul said in 1 Corinthians 14:18, "I thank God that I speak in tongues more than all of you." Could praying in the Spirit be one of the reasons he received amazing revelations from the Spirit of God? I believe it was. You can only enjoy the benefits of a spiritual download if you continue to use your prayer language. Praying in the Spirit opens your valve to receive revelation and understanding from God. That is why it is so important to learn to mediate on scriptures from your daily devotions.

God's Photo Album

I've joined the honored ranks of the proud Grandma Club. Every grandmother thinks she has the most wonderful grandchildren in the entire world. If I wanted you to know my grandchildren, I could tell you how old they are. I could tell you their names. I could tell you stories about them. I could tell you stories that detail their beauty and intellect. I could describe the color of their hair and eyes. I could even reach into my purse and pull out pictures of them. Would you know them then? No. But, the oral description and the picture would help you recognize them.

That's what the Bible has done. The Bible contains numerous portraits that describe the personality of precious Holy Spirit. Let me show you some biblical metaphors that describe precious Holy Spirit.

WIND

Like the wind, you cannot see Him. "...the Spirit of truth. The world cannot accept him, because it neither sees him nor knows him. But you know him, for he lives with you and will be in you." (John 14:17 NIV) He is a spirit. Even though we can't see Him, we will know Him. He will be with us and dwell within us. Alexander Cruden explains:

> The Holy Ghost is called "spirit," being as it were, breathed, and proceeding from the Father and the Son, who inspire and move our hearts by Him; or, because He breatheth where He listeth; stirring up spiritual motions in the hearts

Promised-Gift

of believers, purifying and quickening them; or because He is spiritual, visible and incorporeal essence.[34]

DOVE

Like a dove, Holy Spirit is gentle and sensitive. Jesus asked John to baptize Him. When Jesus came up out of the water, the Spirit of God came down like a dove and sat on Him. First, this was a sign to John so He would recognize Jesus as the Messiah, but it is also descriptive of the nature of precious Holy Spirit. (Matthew 3:16) He is gentle like a dove. He isn't pushy and loud. His voice comes from within your spirit. His leading is gentle. He shows you the way, but He doesn't make you do it. You don't need to be afraid of Him any more than you would a beautiful, little dove.

TEACHER

Holy Spirit is like a teacher. "But when the Father sends the Counselor as my representative -- and by the Counselor I mean the Holy Spirit -- he will teach you everything and will remind you of everything I myself have told you." (John 14:26) Do you think "he will teach you everything" includes ordinary things? Do you think Holy Spirit could teach you how to be a better husband/wife, teacher, or engineer? Do you think He could teach you to grow a better garden or give you an idea for a company or invention? Last time I checked, everything really means everything.

COMFORTER

In John 15:26 (KJV), Holy Spirit is called Comforter, and like a comforter (blanket), He consoles, comforts, calms, and soothes. In times of trouble, run to God; allow Him to wrap you in the soft blanket of His love and whisper peace into your spirit. Don't run from Him; run to Him.

---

[34] Dr. Herbert Lockyear, *All the Doctrines of the Bible*, 1964, Zondervan Publishing House Grand Rapids, Michigan p.74.

ADVOCATE

(John 15:26) The word, paraclete, is translated as "comforter" in the King James Version, but it also means "advocate," as translated in the New Living Translation. A person who has been bullied can really understand this word, advocate, better than most. An advocate is someone who stands up for you, like a strong man stands up for a little kid being bullied, or a brilliant attorney stands with his accused client before a judge. The feeling of hopelessness can be debilitating when you face a giant problem without the resources or reasoning to defend yourself. Or, the flood of relief that comes when a powerful friend moves to your side to defend and protect you is like breathing fresh air into your lungs after a deep dive in water.

GUIDE

(John 16:13) Like a GPS tells and shows a driver the best route to take to reach the destination, precious Holy Spirit is your personal guide. He sees more than a map. He sees God's perfect plan for your life. He sees the future. He knows what is best and directs us toward it.

Issaac Hoopii is a good example of how Holy Spirit guides us. He was a Pentagon police officer when the Pentagon was hit on 9-11. Amidst the smoky confusion and burning debris, he called into the flames, "Come to my voice." Then, he carefully guided the victims to safety.[35]

Trinity

Before I continue this discourse on Holy Spirit, let me establish that I am not talking about another God. We are only focusing on the third member of the Godhead. He is not third in rank of importance, but third in revelation sequence. Theologians explain this amalgamation of three distinct personalities into one God as the Trinity. The Trinity

---

[35]http://www.loc.gov/loc/lcib/0201/olymp-utah.htm (accessed June 1, 2011)

Promised-Gift

is an additional example of God's nature, which leaves human intellect baffled. I wonder if God chuckles sometimes when even the most brilliant minds try to explain His secrets. While I don't understand the how, I do recognize the reality that we worship one God, eternally resident in three distinct persons. "We worship one God in Trinity, and Trinity in Unity," confessing that "the Father is God, the Son is God, and the Holy Ghost is God; and yet they are not three Gods, but one God."[36]

I want to introduce the reality of Holy Spirit, so you can enjoy a greater fullness of God in your life. If a package arrived, but you didn't see or know anything about the package, you couldn't enjoy its contents. Even if you really needed and wanted what was inside the package, you would not enjoy the benefits because you didn't know it had arrived for you.

God sent His marvelous gift, precious Holy Spirit; however, the reality of precious Holy Spirit seems to be missing in the modern church. We know a lot about God the Father, because God gave us natural fathers to give us a glimmer of the Father's nature. We see Father God's omnipotent power demonstrated, as He spoke all of creation into existence. Because Jesus, the living Word, was clothed with flesh and walked with real people, we have numerous descriptions and stories of Him. It is because of His sinless life, His atoning death, and His resurrection that we can be born again. We stop there, neglecting, even ignoring, the role of the third person of the Trinity in the church and in our lives. Could that be the reason we struggle to win over sin? Could our ignorance be the source of our barrenness and ineffectiveness? We were born of the Spirit. When we fail to live by the Spirit, which is the breath of God, we languish. We gasp for more, like a fish out of water.

"God the Father chose you long ago, and the Spirit has made you holy. As a result, you have obeyed Jesus Christ and are cleansed by his blood. May you have more and more of God's special favor and wonderful peace." (1 Peter 1:2) Here we see distinct activities taking

---

[36] Clark, *The Paraclete*, 34.

place: the Father planning; Holy Spirit sanctifying; and Jesus redeeming. "May the grace of our Lord Jesus Christ, the love of God, and the fellowship of the Holy Spirit be with you all." (2 Corinthians 13:13) In this verse, specific roles are assigned. We see the Father loving, the Son saving, and Holy Spirit fellowshipping.

The Bible gives us a quick peek at each member of Trinity in attendance at the baptism of Jesus. Holy Spirit, in the form of a Dove, is seen resting on Jesus; Jesus, the Son, is obeying; and the Father is speaking "...This is my beloved Son..." (Matthew 3:17) Even mankind's redemption is a cooperative function in which the Father outlined the plan of salvation. The Son purchased our redemption through His sacrifice on the cross. Holy Spirit draws mankind to repentance. "Thus the order of divine performance is, from the Father- through the Son - by the Spirit."[37]

Filter of Your Understanding

While I make good biscuits, nobody makes biscuits like my mama. I was awakened on countless mornings by the sound of my mom whacking the sifter on the side of her big metal biscuit pan. The sound of her turning the crank on the sifter around and around announced there would be delicious biscuits coming out of the oven soon. The sifter fluffed the flour and pushed the small, smooth grains of flour through the tiny holes. The larger, hard lumps remained in the sifter to be thrown away.

Sifting the flour makes great biscuits, but it's crazy when we try to do the same thing with God. We try to sift everything – what we see in Scripture and what we experience - through the sieve of our understanding. Everything that God wants to do in our life will not fit through the tiny holes of our understanding. God is bigger than our understanding. We will miss so much, if we wait until we understand before we receive. We will never understand everything God does. His ways are higher than our ways.

---

[37] Dr. Herbert Lockyear, *All the Doctrines of the Bible*, 1964, Zondervan Publishing House Grand Rapids, Michigan p.75.

Following God when I don't understand requires me to use a larger filter; a filter of questions that helps me see the person behind the voice. Do I see the nature of God in this? What is God speaking to me? Does this contradict the Word of God? Does it make me want to be more like Jesus? Does it make me want to serve others more?

We must use the filter of faith instead of fear. I don't understand how God's Spirit can fill us. I don't understand how His wisdom and ability can energize and invigorate me; but, if I fail to believe, then I fail to receive all that God has for me. I don't want that to happen, so I must examine Scripture. I must pray with the confidence that the God of all light will guide me, just as Issaac Hoopii guided employees trapped in the Pentagon. Use your faith filter.

Acts 19:1-6

Almost twenty years had passed since the mighty outpouring at Pentecost. Paul was on one of his trips. He would never be content to allow Pentecost to fade into a distant memory. He kept the fire going in his heart by praying in tongues regularly. "I thank God that I speak in tongues more than all of you." (1 Corinthians 14:18) Paul traveled, encouraging believers and churches as a spiritual father and leader. One of his missionary stops was Ephesus. There was a church of believers there.

> [1]While Apollos was in Corinth, Paul traveled through the interior provinces. Finally, he came to Ephesus, where he found several believers. [2]"Did you receive the Holy Spirit when you believed?" he asked them. "No," they replied, "we don't know what you mean. We haven't even heard that there is a Holy Spirit." [3]"Then what baptism did you experience?" he asked. And they replied, "The baptism of John." [4]Paul said, "John's baptism was to demonstrate a desire to turn from sin and turn to God. John himself told the people to believe in Jesus, the one John said would come later." [5]As soon as they heard this, they were baptized in the name of the Lord Jesus.

Pentecost Lost

> ⁶Then when Paul laid his hands on them, the Holy Spirit came on them, and they spoke in other tongues and prophesied.
>
> ---Acts 19:1-6

Paul asked them, "Did you receive the Holy Spirit when you believed?" They were already believers because they had repented of their sins and believed on Christ Jesus, but they had not received the gift of Holy Spirit.

I love what happened next. Paul laid hands on them, and they had their personal Pentecost. Twenty years had passed, but the flames of Pentecost had not burned out. They never will. When Paul laid hands on them, they did the same thing the believers at Pentecost did, they spoke with tongues. The Ephesian believers spoke with tongues, and they also prophesied. Being filled with Holy Spirit is the doorway into the other gifts of the Spirit.

I want to ask you the same question Paul asked the Ephesian believers, "Did you receive the Holy Spirit when you believed?" If you have received, I encourage you to use your prayer language on a daily basis. It takes the same faith to use your prayer language as it does to receive it. Allow Holy Spirit to flow through you with words coming from your lips that you do not understand. If you have not received since you believed, lay aside your guilt, your doubts, and your opinion and receive the infilling of precious Holy Spirit.

It Keeps on Giving

The outpouring of Holy Spirit on the Day of Pentecost did not end when the day was over. There are numerous accounts of the infilling and empowerment of Holy Spirit in both the Book of Acts and the Pauline epistles. Any understanding of the Spirit's work that is limited to regeneration alone is not representative of the biblical record. A few of my favorites include: Acts 8:17; Acts 9:17; Acts 10:44−46; Acts 19:4−7; Romans 1:11; 1 Corinthians 12−14; Ephesians 5:18−21; 1 Thessalonians 5:19, 20; Hebrews 2:4.

Benefits

- **Spirit Builder:** "I pray that from his glorious, unlimited resources he will give you mighty inner strength through his Holy Spirit." (Ephesians 3:16)

- **Power to Witness:** "But when the Holy Spirit has come upon you, you will receive power and will tell people about me everywhere -- in Jerusalem, throughout Judea, in Samaria, and to the ends of the earth." (Acts 1:8)

- **Joy:** "And the believers were filled with joy and with the Holy Spirit" (Acts 13:52)

- **Righteousness, Peace and Joy:** "For the Kingdom of God is not a matter of what we eat or drink, but of living a life of goodness and peace and joy in the Holy Spirit." (Romans 14:17)

- **Hope, Joy and Peace**: "So I pray that God, who gives you hope, will keep you happy and full of peace as you believe in him. May you overflow with hope through the power of the Holy Spirit." (Romans 15:13)

- **Helps our weakness**: "And the Holy Spirit helps us in our distress. For we don't even know what we should pray for, nor how we should pray. But the Holy Spirit prays for us with groanings that cannot be expressed in words." (Romans 8:26)

You Must Want the Gift

Have you ever yelled to your kids, "Has anybody seen my car keys?" Yeah, I thought so. And then, your next comment is, "Help me look for my keys, please."

But, they're not worried. As a matter of fact, they grumble as they half-heartedly look under the edge of their chair and yell back, "Can't find them, Mom!" They don't need the keys, so their search is careless and quick.

Suddenly, the scene changes when they receive an invitation to their friends house to play the new release of their favorite video game. They ask you to take them to their friends. Now you say, "Has anybody seen my car keys?" Suddenly, they turn into some kind of super hero. They speed through the house like the comic character, "Flash", overturning the furniture with the strength of Superman, looking for those keys.

What changed? Their desire changed. Suddenly, they were desperate to find the keys! Their actions were influenced by their personal desperation.

You must want more of God and pursue Him like kids seek their mom's keys when they want to go somewhere special. Most of us seek God when it is convenient or easy. We must search for Him, like a thirsty deer searches for water on a hot day. We must become desperate for Him, like a fisherman bailing water out of his boat to keep it from sinking. He wants us to lovingly pursue him, like we would scour every inch of our neighborhood for our lost puppy. We must desire Him, like a treasure hunter digs for lost treasure. God wants us to seek Him like a hungry hunter who needs to feed his family would seek game. When we seek God, when we search desperately for Him, we will find Him. "If you look for me in earnest, you will find me when you seek me." (Jeremiah 29:13)

I am not inferring that God is lost or that He is hiding from you. God has promised that He is always with you. Still, His manifest presence must be sought to be experienced. He wants you to "feel" His presence. "His purpose in all of this was that the nations should seek after God and perhaps feel their way toward him and find him -- though he is not far from any one of us." (Acts 17:27) God doesn't hide Himself from you. He hides Himself for you. He hides Himself, like He hid gold or diamonds in the earth. His presence is better than gold. In His presence is fullness of joy! Learn to enjoy His presence. While we must never be disrespectful or dishonoring in any fashion, we can relax when we talk to God. That should include your worship.

Some people are not comfortable saying, "I love you" to God, or whispering worship aloud to God. Push past your feelings by increasing your private worship. Ask God to heal any deep-seated emotions that may hinder your worship.

Don't try to exempt yourself from worship with excuses like: I'm just not the type to worship; I can't worship to that music; I'm too shy to raise my hands in public. It's not about you. Pride is a sin. Repent, humble yourself, and obey the biblical template of praise and worship.

Worship opens your spirit for God's manifest presence and the infilling of the Holy Spirit. I don't always feel something when I worship. When I don't feel His presence, I ask God to search my heart, "Father, is there any sin in my heart?" If He reminds me of something, I repent. If Holy Spirit doesn't remind me of sin, then I intensify my worship instead of quitting. During those times that I don't sense His presence, I listen more closely to hear His voice. Most of the time, God chooses quiet times to talk to me.

Although I love to feel His presence, the objective of my worship is more than experiencing an emotional charge. My goal is to honor God by expressing my love through worship. To adequately express my love, I must know Him well enough to know what He enjoys. Sometimes I ask God, "How do you want me to worship you? Show me how to worship you in a way that is pleasing to you." Or, I use worship models patterned by the psalmists in the Bible. I kneel or lay prostrate with my face on the floor. Sometimes, I sway from side to side. At other times, I just stand with my hands raised in surrender. I have discovered, if I seek Him, I will find Him. Sincere and deep worship is a vital key to receiving the infilling of the Holy Spirit.

Accept Your Gift

"Through the work of Christ Jesus, God has blessed the Gentiles with the same blessing he promised to Abraham, and we Christians receive the promised Holy Spirit through faith." (Galatians 3:14)

Pentecost Lost

When a man falls in love with a woman and wants to marry her, he offers her a gift to express His love - an engagement ring. But, sometimes a woman will not accept the gift! Ouch!

Have you ever given a gift to someone, and they didn't want it? I have! They even gave it back to me. Ouch! Your gift of Holy Spirit has arrived. As with any other gift, you must either accept it or refuse it.

Too many people, without actually saying the words, refuse to accept the gift of Holy Spirit. Some people want the gift, but they don't want to speak in tongues. Some people have traditions and beliefs that hinder them from receiving God's gift. There are some Christians who refuse because they are just content or uninterested in receiving more of God.

Sometimes people rationalize, "If God wanted me to have the gift, I would already have it." Or, they may say, "If God wants me to have it, then He can just give it to me." I've even heard, "I asked God one time for Holy Spirit, and nothing happened; so, it must not be for me." The problem with that thinking is that God has already given Holy Spirit. We have a free will to accept, or refuse His gift. We must make the choice. We cannot remain neutral. The choice is simply receive or refuse.

How to Receive

It is easy to receive a gift from a giver you can see; you simply reach your hand out and take the gift. You can't see Holy Spirit, so how do you receive Him?

Ask

"If you sinful people know how to give good gifts to your children, how much more will your heavenly Father give the Holy Spirit to those who ask him." (Luke 11:13) Don't beg, plead or whine. Just ask Him to fill you with Holy Spirit.

Receive By Faith

"Through the work of Christ Jesus, God has blessed the Gentiles with the same blessing he promised to Abraham, and we Christians receive the promised Holy Spirit through faith." (Galatians 3:14)

Just as you received Jesus as your Savior through faith, receive Holy Spirit by faith. Believe that God will do what He promised. Believe that you will receive. Banish all fear and doubt from your mind by focusing on Jesus. Your mind can wander, so begin to worship Jesus deliberately and aloud. Focus on expressing your love to Jesus, and progress from just thanking Jesus to worshipping Him from deep within your spirit. Your focus is not on receiving a gift. Your focus is on Jesus, the baptizer.

When a woman accepts an engagement ring, she's receiving more than a ring. Yes, she will enjoy the ring, but she is more excited about gaining a husband than the ring on her finger. We should approach God in the same way. Worship Him from the deepest part of your being! Sincerely express your love aloud. It is important that you give voice to your praise. Relax, but open your mouth and speak your worship.

Yield

When soft, pliable clay is shaped in your hands, it yields to your touch, doing what your fingers guide it to do. But, if you leave the clay out to harden, it refuses to be shaped or formed, and instead it crumbles in your hands.

As you worship, yield to Him. Precious Holy Spirit will give you words or sounds to speak. A new partnership with Holy Spirit is formed. He supplies the words, and by faith and obedience, you speak the words. The words will come from deep within your spirit and seem to bubble up into your mind. Sometimes, people's lips will begin to tremble. If that happens to you, deliberately speak the sounds out.

Pentecost Lost

I am about to share a very simple, but important key that many people overlook. "And everyone present was filled with the Holy Spirit and began speaking in other languages, as the Holy Spirit gave them this ability." (Acts 2:4) In this verse, who spoke? Read it carefully. They spoke. Holy Spirit gave the words. It is important to understand that God is not going to make your lips move. He is not going to make you speak in tongues. It is a partnership. He supplies the words. You speak them out.

What Will Happen?

Often, people want to know what will happen when they receive Holy Spirit infilling! I find that each person reacts differently, just like people respond differently to simple things, like watching a movie. Some people laugh loudly at every little thing, while others only smile slightly at the most hilarious comedy.

Receiving Holy Spirit is absolutely a supernatural experience. Yet, it is not always a spectacular experience. Holy Spirit infilling is more than a feeling. Your goal is not to receive a feeling, but the infilling of Holy Spirit. It is a life-changing experience, not necessarily an emotional one. God's order is always in the following sequence: Fact; Faith; Feeling. Trust God's promise in the Bible, and thank God for its fulfillment, apart from any emotion. "This (speaking of emotions) will assuredly follow, but generally not until we have honored God by relying on His faithfulness, without any special manifestation of the blessing we are seeking."[38]

While reactions do vary from person to person, there is a spiritual pattern that is established from the five initial outpourings recorded in scripture: you will speak with tongues! The scripture references for the five initial outpouring of Holy Spirit are found as follows:

Acts 2;   Acts 8;   Acts 9;   Acts 10;   Acts 19.

---

[38] Harris, *When He is Come*, 82.

Promised-Gift

Amazingly and sadly, I've seen people respond to an invitation to receive the infilling of Holy Spirit, only to stand at the front, looking around. Even after being encouraged to engage in worship, they just stand there, chewing their gum, or with their mouth clamped shut. They stand there as if trying to figure out why God doesn't just zap them with their gift, so they can plop back in their seats. If you want Him, you must participate by opening the door of your spirit with worship. He really is a gentleman. Typically, He doesn't go around breaking down people's doors, so open yours with worship. Worship creates an atmosphere of expectancy and warmth, just like an anxious mama waits at the door to welcome her war-weary soldier son home.

Too often, we want to receive from God on our terms. Suppose I told you I had purchased a gift for you and then gave you the following specific instructions: "Go get your gift. It's under the bed in your room." I would be baffled if, instead of going to your bedroom to get your gift, you started crying and begging me for the gift. Or, what if you opened the refrigerator and the kitchen cabinets and then went outside and climbed a tree looking for your gift? That's ridiculous. If you believed me, you would retrieve your gift from under the bed.

Is God any less credible? You've got to go where the gift is. You will find God's gift in the giver--Jesus. Jesus is the baptizer. The way into His presence is worship. Scripture clearly explains how to enter His presence. "Enter his gates with thanksgiving; go into his courts with praise. Give thanks to him and bless his name." (Psalms 100:4)

Un-wrap your Gift

I can never remember my dad opening a gift - not a birthday present, not a Christmas present, not any present, ever. When I begged him to open his gift, he would offer a glib, "Thank you. I'll open it later." I assume he opened my gifts, but I never saw him do it, nor would he ever explain why. My desire to give him something he would enjoy was futile if he refused to open it. The fullest benefit is only realized as the gift is opened and used.

Unwrapping God's gift is more of a relationship development than a one-time event. There are no shortcuts in relationship building; you must spend time with Him to discover who He is, and who He wants to be in your life.

Enjoy the benefits of your Gift

Items are often purchased in package deals. You agree to purchase a cell phone plan for two years, and they give you a free phone. You buy a digital camera, and it comes with a battery charger. Few people realize that God includes a benefit package with Holy Spirit infilling. One benefit He included is your personal prayer language to keep your spirit man charged. "I pray that from his glorious, unlimited resources he will give you mighty inner strength through his Holy Spirit." (Ephesians 3:16) Praying in tongues is more than an initial evidence to confirm that you received His gift. It is your prayer language to use freely. Praying in tongues is an awesome benefit! I recommend that you use it daily.

Think about it:
_____

DUI: Dwell Under the Influence

Dear God, What do you want me to take away from this chapter?

Have you received God's Promised Gift?

Are you enjoying God's Gift?

Chapter Four

Partner- Wind

Let's Go Sailing

The sunlight reflects and dances on the emerald green water like diamonds as the sailboat glides across the water. The wind blows through your hair as the birds sing and squawk overhead. You just can't beat sailing. Let's do it; let's go sailing. With the decision made, you go through all the preparation: getting ready, renting a boat, packing the car, unloading the car, and finally loading everything into the boat. You are tired, but ready to set sail for the adventure that lies ahead. After hoisting the sails, your heart suddenly sinks. The sailboat sits motionless on the glassy water because there is no wind. All your plans and all your efforts are futile because you must have wind to sail. The strongest muscles and the best strategies cannot put wind in the sails.

Sometimes, I can identify with the person I just described. Sometimes, spiritually, I feel like I have done everything I know to do, and it was all pointless. Sometimes, I feel like saying "God, I could use some help here." Sometimes, He says back to me, "I was waiting for you to ask." We may not perceive the desperation of our need, yet the fact remains: we need His help. "Then he said to me, 'This is what the LORD says to Zerubbabel: It is not by force nor by strength, but by my Spirit, says the LORD Almighty.'" (Zechariah 4:6)

Our need doesn't take God by surprise. In fact, He planned ahead and sent us a helper, or a partner, to put the wind in our sails, so we can do and be all that He planned for us. That partner is Holy Spirit. He came to partner with us and to help us put processes in place that position us for blessing.

Partner - Wind

Wind Power

I love the beach for many reasons. I have always loved to feel the squish of wet sand under my feet. I love to watch the sea oats swaying back and forth in the summer breeze and watch the sea gulls squawking and fighting over a cheese curl. But now, I have a new favorite: watching kite surfers! Kite surfing, or kite boarding, is a surface water sport that uses wind power to pull a rider through the water on a small surfboard or a kite board (similar to a wakeboard). This intriguing sport attracted 150,000 people in 2006. What an adrenal rush that must be - to cruise across the water using wind power.[39] It is hard to imagine the power that propels a kite surfer across the surface of bumpy waves, as if pushing a small toy. The sail is stretched taunt by the winds that fill and push it across the sky, like a bully shoving a fragile child. The sail is attached to the surfer's body with a heavy-duty harness. A surfer, using a control bar, can crisscross the waves on a kite board.

The howling sound, like that of a mighty wind, was the precursor of the change that was about to take place. Just as the aftermath of high wind is substantiated by change, the wake of Pentecost is evidenced by changed lives. Not only were the 120 believers who received the gift of Holy Spirit revolutionized, but the powerful demonstration that unbelievers heard and saw produced 3,000 new converts. The power of the wind of the Spirit, God's gift, produced boldness in Peter, and its ripple effect brought Pentecost to believers, unconstrained by boundaries of gender or race. To Saul, God brought sight and insight; even his name was changed to Paul. To Barnabas, it brought guidance and the courage to act on that guidance. The wind of Pentecost expanded the scope of miracles and healings.

The outpouring of Holy Spirit on the day of Pentecost was more than an historical event. It was and is the fulfillment of a promise: that He would send Holy Spirit into the world after His ascension to heaven. He promised that Holy Spirit would be with us and in us.

---

[39]http://en.wikipedia.org/wiki/Kitesurfing (accessed June 2, 2011)

Pentecost Lost

Precious Holy Spirit fills us like the wind fills the surfer's sail at the beach, enabling them to surf. Precious Holy Spirit's power enables us to do all the things that are part of real Christian living. He gives us power to win over sin and power to witness. He shares God's secrets with us and helps us know Jesus better. God wants to display His nature and works in our modern culture through the life and activities of a Spirit-filled believer.

Wind, by its very nature, is moving. Holy Spirit, by His very nature, is active: moving, changing things, creating things, and uncovering things. You cannot push Him into a dark corner, a closet in the basement of your life, or behind a locked door and still expect Spirit-filled results in your life. Allow Him to move in your life to shape you into the image of Christ.

Holy Spirit

Some people stumble over His name, Holy Spirit, (or Holy Ghost as found in the King James Version). People stop short without knowing Him because His name conjures up pictures of spooky, creepy things or haunted buildings. When this teaching is done, I hope the word "Spirit" will convey a new, precious, and glorious picture instead.

His name means wind or breath. Pneuma is the Greek word for spirit. It shows up 385 times in the New Testament. In almost every language, "wind or breath" is a synonym for spirit. Wind (moving air) is a symbol of life. The first thing we ask after an accident is "Are they breathing?" The wind mirrors the personality of Holy Spirit. We could use "Holy Breath or Holy Life" to describe His personality. Dr. Lockyear explains, "As human breath, which is the word used for "spirit," is an invisible part of man, and represents his vitality, his life and energy, so the Spirit of God and of Christ is so designated because He is "breathed forth" or given by both for the accomplishment of their mutual purpose in and through man. The

Partner - Wind

Spirit is "The breath of God.""[40] Holy Spirit breathes life into a believer; He refreshes and renews the heart of a believer; just like a breeze on a scorching summer day. He fills us with joy.

While building a log home in the mountains of North Carolina, Wayne and I endured some very hot summer days. Since the air conditioning wasn't installed, we couldn't cool off inside, so we would search for a cool breeze on the wrap-around porch. We have fond memories of sipping sweet, iced tea together on the back porch, while watching the birds soar and glide effortlessly on the wind currents that formed over the valley and brought the cool breezes that refreshed our weary bodies.

While I can't see the wind, I can see and feel its effects. I see the leaves wave in the trees as the wind blows through them. I hear the rattle of trash cans tumbling when overturned by a gust of wind. While I can't see the air that a newborn baby breathes, its welcomed cry announces the presence of both air and life. I'm confident that you would confirm the reality of air, and I hope you'll discover personally the reality of precious Holy Spirit. You cannot see Him with your eyes, but you can feel His presence and enjoy the benefits His infilling brings into your life.

I enjoyed another benefit of the wind one day after I burned some popcorn. Alright, so I have burned popcorn more than once. While I've learned to eat burned popcorn, I hate the horrible smell that fills the house. My kids always thought the smoke alarm was a dinner bell to announce that supper was ready. I'm just teasing! I'm a great cook. Just because my kids desperately included "Make it good, Lord!" in their mealtime prayer doesn't mean I'm not a great cook. So, as I was saying before my humble confession, I have learned through the years to open the windows on both sides of the house to allow a fresh breeze to sweep the horrible smell of burned food out of the house. A fresh wind through open windows will force stale, polluted air out of a room, replacing it with sweet, fresh air.

---

[40] Lockyear, *All the Doctrines of the Bible,* 74.

Pentecost Lost

Yes, Holy Spirit is like a wind. William Robinson Clark said, "But a greater and more effectual purifier is He who is symbolized by the wind, for He can banish the infection of evil, and drive away the pestilence of sin from the hearts and wills of men."[41]

Look at Romans 8:13: "For if you keep on following it, you will perish. But if through the power of the Holy Spirit you turn from it and its evil deeds, you will live." The "it" referred to in this verse is sin. Did you see that? How do we stop sin? Read it again; this is too powerful to miss. We stop sin dead in its tracks through the power of Holy Spirit.

Yes, Holy Spirit is like a gentle breeze and a powerful wind. Living in hurricane country, I've seen powerful winds topple enormous oak trees. I've seen boats tossed inland, like a child tossing a toy. My mother saw a pine needle driven into a solid wood board, just like you would drive a nail; strange but true. Powerful winds bring change; but when it ceases to move, it is no longer wind. William Robinson Clark says:

> And what was the sign by which the heavenly presence was declared? It was "as of the rushing of a mighty wind," one of the most powerful agencies in nature, and one which leaves behind it the most remarkable traces of its influence. The wind is a mighty power; it tears up and casts down the mightiest trees of the forest; it raises the waters of the sea into heaps and mountains, and opens up its depths to the eyes of men. The Spirit of whom it is a symbol is a spirit of power, a mighty agent, Who comes with a new and unknown strength to change the face of humanity and to stir it to its depths."[42]

Like a wind, Holy Spirit brings change. You cannot stay the same in the presence of His wind. He comes to make you more like God. Because Jesus is Truth, one of the primary jobs of your partner, Holy Spirit, is to help you know Jesus better. He will point things out to

---

[41] Clark, *The Paraclete*, 108.
[42] Clark, *The Paraclete*, 107.

you, like a tour guide shows you interesting buildings and landmarks on a trip. "But I will send you the Counselor -- the Spirit of truth. He will come to you from the Father and will tell you all about me." (John 15:26)

Help?

Help? Saul[43] didn't need any help! At least, he didn't realize he needed any! He felt adequately prepared for the task at hand. Saul knew the Scriptures, having studied under the greatest teacher of his time. He knew three languages and embraced the traditions of the strictest Jewish sect. He was well respected, both in his community and by the religious leaders. He was confident, articulate, and powerful!

Jewish religious leaders, including the passionate Saul, considered the new church and teachings of Christ a false religion or cult. The frightened church scattered in all directions, escaping to save their lives. The new faith that glimmered in their hearts was shaken but still alive.

Undaunted by the arduous 150 mile journey, Saul approached Damascus spewing menacing threats, which were sanctioned by the legal search warrant he clutched. With bulldog tenacity, Saul pursued the believers of Christ to arrest them and place them in prison for their perceived heresy.

Suddenly, a powerful light from heaven leveled Saul's pride and posture into a crumpled heap in the middle of a dusty road outside Damascus. His frightened "Who art thou, Lord?" melted into a submissive "What do you want me to do?" Heaven's spotlight closed his eyesight but opened his insight. Suddenly, he saw his need -- Truth. "I am Jesus," the voice from the bright light answered Saul. They all heard it! Saul suddenly saw that religion and self-sufficiency had blinded him to the truth. Now, instead of Saul being the leader,

---

[43] Acts 9:1-20

he needed one. His bewildered followers led him to the home of Judas on Straight Street, where he was able to get a room to stay.

Perhaps desperate and bewildered, Saul replayed the encounter in his personal darkness. Over and over, he must have heard the voice, "I am Jesus!" He prayed, and he fasted. Whirling in confusion, God brought hope with a vivid vision. Don't let the thoughts of having a vision alarm you.

A vision shouldn't be menacing. It is a picture, scene, or movie you see with the eyes of your spirit. It leaves the same imprint on your mind that your eyes typically leave when you look around. In Saul's vision, a man named Ananias came into the room, prayed for him, and then he regained his sight. For three days and three nights, he didn't eat a single bite. He prayed and waited.

It shouldn't be surprising that God was talking to Ananias as well, but Ananias was surprised. Ananias was not an apostle but simply an ordinary, spirit-filled believer to whom God gave succinct instructions: name, address, and phone number. Sorry, it hadn't been invented yet - no phone number - but you can be sure God had Saul's number. Notice the precise instructions that God gave Ananias:

> The Lord said, "Go over to Straight Street, to the house of Judas. When you arrive, ask for Saul of Tarsus. He is praying to me right now. [12]I have shown him a vision of a man named Ananias coming in and laying his hands on him so that he can see again."[13]"But Lord," exclaimed Ananias, "I've heard about the terrible things this man has done to the believers in Jerusalem! [14]And we hear that he is authorized by the leading priests to arrest every believer in Damascus." [15]But the Lord said, "Go and do what I say. For Saul is my chosen instrument to take my message to the Gentiles and to kings, as well as to the people of Israel. (Acts 9:11-15)

God's instructions were alarming, but Ananias moved beyond his reservations to obey. Ananias was a godly man sent to help Saul, but Saul needed help beyond Ananias' ability. He needed more than sight...he needed precious Holy Spirit. Ananias recognized the core need, so He introduced Saul to Holy Spirit.

Ananias placed his hands on Saul and said, "Brother Saul, the Lord, Jesus, who appeared to you on the road as you were coming here has sent me so that you may see again and be filled with Holy Spirit." Immediately, something like scales fell from Saul's eyes. Now he could see. But now his eyesight included both his natural and spiritual vision. His spiritual darkness, confusion, and religious tradition had been shattered by Jesus, the Light of the World.

Transformed, Saul was baptized with more than water. Saul had a new helper, a new purpose, and a new direction. His education was not wasted; he simply had a new lens to view it through. He had a new teacher, precious Holy Spirit. Holy Spirit was also his helper, showing him, guiding him, and opening his eyes, so he could see how Jesus fit and finished the puzzle of Scripture.

God told Ananias "he is a chosen vessel." But Saul's reputation painted him as a menacing enemy rather than someone God could use; yet, through the power of Holy Spirit, Saul became that special container that God saw. "But this precious treasure -- this light and power that now shine within us -- is held in perishable containers, that is, in our weak bodies. So everyone can see that our glorious power is from God and is not our own." (2 Corinthians 4:7)

While Scripture does not indicate here that Saul spoke in tongues when he received Holy Spirit, we do know that he spoke with tongues. Saul, whose name was changed to Paul, emphasizes that point in 1 Corinthians 14:18: "I thank God that I speak in tongues more than all of you."

His gifting and abilities alone were not sufficient to complete God's plan. His powerful relationships and vast knowledge, without The Revealer of Truth, produced sterile legalism. Just as the prophets and writers of the Old Testament, Paul's revelation did not come from the reservoir of his personal knowledge, but its source was precious Holy Spirit. "Above all, you must understand that no prophecy in Scripture ever came from the prophets themselves [21]or because they wanted to prophesy. It was the Holy Spirit who moved the prophets to speak from God." (2 Peter 1: 20, 21)

Pentecost Lost

Why did Paul receive so much revelation knowledge? Did his revelation knowledge come because he used the key given at Pentecost to access the reservoir of God's knowledge? Was praying in tongues his direct link to revelation knowledge? I believe it was the critical link.

We observe the habits of great men to discover reproducible clues, so we can duplicate that greatness in our lives. Paul accessed the Father repeatedly; using his heaven-augmented and heaven-amplified language - augmented and amplified, not in the sense of volume, but in respect to intensity and power. As Paul prayed in his heavenly language, Holy Spirit downloaded revelation knowledge into his spirit and unzipped his understanding, so his mind could receive it as well. Paul did what God called him to do: start churches and disciple believers. He accomplished his objective through speaking, preaching, and writing letters. I don't think he knew his act of obedience would end up in the Bible, which would influence believers for centuries. He just fulfilled the call of God that was on his life.

Knowledge is power. Paul learned to listen to the voice of Holy Spirit as He spoke from the resources of all knowledge. But, somehow, the modern church seems to think we don't need to listen, and it has produced anemic believers. Holy Spirit is not a silent partner. He has a voice, and we must consciously lean closer to hear His voice. Praying in the Spirit helps us to hear more clearly. It unlocks our comprehension, so what we hear becomes reality instead of hollow syllables.

I have discovered that speaking and praying in tongues is a valuable tool in my personal life. I believe it is a biblical process that will enable believers to tap into the resources of heaven. God craves relationship with His children, but you cannot have relationship without communication.

Speaking in Tongues

The wind is a mystery to me but not to meteorologists. They understand the complexities of the wind well enough to forecast wind patterns and wind speeds. How have they unlocked this mystery? They observe the wind. They watch carefully. They deliberately record data. They analyze what they see, investigating the data and patterns, even when the facts challenge their expectations.

Sincere people fail to make that kind of investigation in regards to precious Holy Spirit. When the Scripture doesn't fit into the nice little box of their personal experience or denominational thinking, they choose to explain it away or ignore it completely. Yes, the work of Holy Spirit is a mystery. He is so mind boggling that only God can open our eyes and un-warp our understanding. Set aside your preconceived ideas. Look at scripture honestly, and desperately crave more of Him. Ask Him to open your understanding.

Our conversation on speaking in tongues raises another point of painful contention. Even sincere committed believers stumble over speaking in tongues. They want more of God, but they don't want tongues; or, they do not believe speaking in tongues is for today. Yet, the book of Jude is part of Holy Scripture, and it encourages you to build yourselves up by praying in tongues: "But ye, beloved, building up yourselves on your most holy faith, praying in the Holy Ghost." (Jude 1:20) He was talking to more than apostles; he was talking to all God's beloved, including future generations: "Wherefore, brethren, covet to prophesy, and forbid not to speak with tongues." (1Corinthians 14:39) Speaking in tongues is a gift intended for the modern church. Paul clearly instructed in Scripture that it should not be forbidden. Because believers ignore this simple truth, the church is scrawny and uninspiring.

Every believer can and should be filled with precious Holy Spirit, with the evidence of speaking in tongues. New converts can be filled immediately after conversion, if they are birthed in a climate that welcomes Him and teaches that God has more for them to receive.

Pentecost Lost

Speaking in tongues is a supernatural sign that God, not us, is in control. It is a reminder that our God wants to help us worship and pray. That influence and assistance will begin to trickle into every other area of our life as well. James 3:5-8 explains that, although our tongue is a little member, its influence and power is enormous. He compares the tongue to a rudder that directs the course of our life. That is why He wants us to surrender our tongue to Him by praying in the Spirit. When we surrender our tongue to God, our thoughts, attitudes, and actions are influenced by that surrender. When we speak in tongues, we are directing the course of our life toward heaven. Speaking in words we do not understand is an activity of surrender.

Carnal pride can cause us to stiffen and resist the strategy of heaven, instead of bowing humbly to receive all that God has for us. We cannot contrive rules that fit our whims if we sincerely crave heaven's best. We must live by God's rule book if we expect to win the race.

While the wind cannot be controlled, its benefits can be harnessed, when you understand the Laws of Aerodynamics. An airplane does not defy these laws. An aeronautical engineer employs the laws to construct a machine that is capable of flying. When you understand the laws associated with the wind, you can tap into its power via windmills to produce electricity or via sails to push boats across the waves of the ocean. Understanding these laws gives a person the ability to partner with the wind to produce a desired effect.

As Holy Spirit reveals the mysteries of God's plan of redemption, we can partner with God's laws to produce the results He hid for us in His original plan. Praying in tongues is one key to unlock the mysteries of God. As we pray in tongues, Holy Spirit will reveal God's plan in our spirit. Sometimes, it will be a thought or a good idea that pops into our mind as we are praying. Jot down the idea, and continue praying. He will guide us in practical ways. "For all who are led by the Spirit of God are children of God." (Romans 8:14)

Ask God to unlock your understanding and help you discover truth. Fall in love with Jesus, and dare to become a worshiper;

worshipping deeply and expressing love with words spoken aloud. You'll discover expressing your love to God causes it to deepen. Your words and worship are powerful. "This message was kept secret for centuries and generations past, but now it has been revealed to his own holy people." (Colossians 1:26)

Learn to listen. You must quiet your spirit long enough to hear His voice. God speaks to your spirit. Pray in tongues often. Be diligent to read the Bible and meditate on what you read. Develop a habit of reading the Bible while you pray quietly in tongues. Use the same diligence to nourish and build your spirit that you do to feed and groom your body.

Paraclete

We've talked about his name, Pnuema. Now let's talk about another cavernous word from the Greek that describes the work of Holy Spirit - Parakletos or Paraclete. It was translated "comforter" in John 14:16 (KJV): "And I will pray the Father, and he shall give you another Comforter, that he may abide with you forever..." I am thankful that the works of Holy Spirit include being a gentle comforter which brings peace in times of trouble and turmoil. Yet, there are six other words that the translators could have used. They include Counselor, Intercessor, Helper, Strengthener, Standby, and Advocate.[44] Each describes a different function He can do in a believer. As advocate or lawyer, He is defending you before your accuser: pleading and arguing your case. As Standby, He is your constant companion, in both bad times and good.

As Strengthener, His strength develops a courageous backbone within you. He wraps you in His strength, like a dad wraps his arms around his little child and places his hands onto the bat to help him smack the ball into outfield. The child taps into strength beyond his own. Each facet of paraclete reflects another dimension of His love and commitment to you.

---

[44] Dr. William Smith, *Smith's Bible Dictionary* 1901 "Entry for 'Advocate'."

Pentecost Lost

Let's look at the prefix of this word, "para," which is used in many English words. Para means side by side. A paralegal is trained to help a lawyer but does not have a license to practice law. A paraprofessional is a professional trained to assist specific professions. Nature exemplifies the benefits of partnerships with schools of fish, hives of bees, packs of wolves, and flocks of birds.

"Cleat" is the English word that is derived from "celte," which means wedge.[45] Football players wear cleats on their shoes to give them leverage and help keep them from slipping and falling when running across the field. Cleats help a player run faster; they grip the turf to enable his hits and throws to be more powerful.

Look closely at this analogy. Scripture is the foundation for every believer. The partnership of Holy Spirit facilitates your efforts to get a grip on the promises of the Bible by revealing truths and by opening your understanding to the reality of those truths in a practical way. He knows that when you grasp scriptural principles, they will keep you from slipping and help you run your race successfully.

But, the wonderful truth is that He doesn't stop by occasionally to help you out. He will be with you all the time. "And I will ask the Father, and he will give you another paraclete (*Comforter, Counselor, Intercessor, Helper, Strengthener, Standby, Advocate*), who will never leave you." (John 14:16) The thought doesn't even stop here. It continues in verse 17: "He is the Holy Spirit, who leads into all truth. The world at large cannot receive him, because it isn't looking for him and doesn't recognize him. But you do, because he lives with you now and later will be in you." I love this metaphor. It is like dipping fabric into dye. The fabric is in the dye, and the dye soaks into the fabric. It is almost too marvelous to grasp that Holy Spirit would dwell, not just with us, but in us.

---

[45]Modern Language Association (MLA):"cleat." *Dictionary.com Unabridged*. Random House, Inc. 14 Sep. 2010. Dictionary.com http://dictionary.reference.com/browse/cleat. (accessed June 1, 2011)

Puppet or Partner

A simple explanation of a paraclete is partner. A partner helps without manipulating. A puppeteer can make his puppet jump up and down, clap its hands, or open its mouth. He can make his puppet look stupid or graceful, all at the puppeteer's personal whim. The puppet has no choice. It can only do what it is forced to do. This is not a picture of a partner.

Unlike a manipulator or puppeteer, a partner steps beside you to help you pull your load, like yoked oxen pull a cart together. A partner assists you by accomplishing what you cannot do. It is a joining of two different parts to make a whole. You do your part, and they do their part. Each partner must do his or her part to complete the partnership. Holy Spirit came to live in you to partner with you. There is a spiritual tension that believers often overlook: either they expect God to do it all or they try to do it all. Neither of these achieves the goal of partnership. God is looking for partnership, not spectatorship or dictatorship. You were made to have relationship with God. He wants you to serve Him from a heart that welcomes and worships Him and not because you are forced. He leaves your will (your right to choose) intact. He doesn't force you, yet the warmth of His presence melts the allure of sin.

The taste of His sweet fellowship stimulates your appetite. The constant direction of that communion is Jesus. Holy Spirit wants to tell you about Jesus, like a skilled and passionate teacher unfolds his or her passion. He wants to disclose deep secrets and reveal Jesus to you in ways you never saw before. You'll fall in love with Jesus. Oh, I know you already love Him, but you'll discover the reality of a deeper love because the more you know Him, the more you'll love Him. The magnitude of that love, loving and being loved, changes you. It changes what you want to do, and what you don't want to do. You will begin to love the things God loves and hate the things God hates. Your life will take on new meaning and purpose as you fervently live to please Him. This transformation is a product of influence, not dictatorship.

Pentecost Lost

It is an astonishing reality that Holy Spirit wants to help you! He wants to help you do great things, but He wants to help you do ordinary things well, also. Often, simple acts of obedience to do ordinary things will enlarge your capacity to experience extraordinary things. I've heard businessmen explain that they hired an employee because his shoes were polished to perfection. Shining his shoes was a little thing that led to a big opportunity. God is concerned about the little things in your life. As you follow the voice of His Spirit, you discover little, daily choices can lead to big victories.

Steam Engine Train

Can you imagine the thrill and excitement that ebbed from settlers as they watched the first steam engines huffing and puffing across the plains and over the mountains? The shrill voice of the whistle broadcast the arrival of the train, while warning people and animals to move off the track. That little whistle was and continues to be a vital communication tool on the train to both warn of impending danger and communicate instructions to linemen and other personnel. While the train was not built for the whistle, it has a vital role on the train.

I want to make it equally clear that Holy Spirit is so multifaceted and so marvelous that the pages of the largest book cannot contain the enormity of who He is, yet one of the benefits of the infilling of Holy Spirit is speaking in tongues. Holy Spirit wants to expand your ability to intercede for the lost and the needs of others through your prayer language. Sometimes I ask Holy Spirit to please help me pray for a specific person, and I begin to pray in tongues. I pray for that person in my mind, while I pray in the Spirit with my voice. If a specific thought of how I should pray comes to mind, I stop praying in tongues and pray in English what I hear in my spirit.

Like the whistle on the train warns of impending danger, the wind of Holy Spirit can flow through you to make you an effective communicator, give you the knowledge needed to warn people of coming destruction, and help you express His love through your

Partner - Wind

personal witness. He craves the opportunity to empower each believer to share His love and the enormity of His grace. When you exalt Him, He is like a magnet; He draws people to Himself. You must not be silent; too much is at stake. It is critical that you allow Holy Spirit to help you witness and touch heaven with the needs of people through intercession.

The voice of the engineer or conductor cannot be heard yelling warnings over the huffing and groaning of the big iron horse. Railroad workers, backing up trains or connecting rail cars, receive warning and instructions via the train whistle. It doesn't seem that sinners want to listen to us. Maybe they can't hear over the noise and roar of our culture. But when a believer speaks with the same anointing that Christ spoke, words cut through the racket to find its place beyond the ear to kiss the heart. Holy Spirit is heaven's agent, releasing conviction that leads to repentance.

I think we fail to be the powerful witnesses God intended because we don't engage the partnership of Holy Spirit in our witnessing efforts. Our words alone remain mere words. Human effort is part of the equation, but only part of it. Yes, we must step out to witness. Yes, we must do our part, but when we fail to recognize the power of partnership, we fail. God's great commission to witness was given to every believer. God's strategy is not flawed; nor will His ability fail. Spirit-empowered witnessing is not some mystical or emotional experience. It is our acknowledgement that we need His help, which causes us to pray in the Spirit to ask for His help and to prepare ourselves to witness. It causes us to look for people who need His love. It causes us to reach beyond our comfort zone to touch humanity's greatest need.

While I am on the subject of trains, I must issue this warning: don't restrict or confine Holy Spirit to the function of only being a whistle in your life. What do I mean? I have seen some Pentecostal believers praying in tongues in church, yet they never seem to have the fruit that should accompany a Spirit-filled believer. I am not that person's judge, but I am looking for ways to help people be more fruitful. I have known people, personally, who refused to forgive the least offense but participated in loud manifestations at church. This observation by many church leaders seems to give credibility to the idea that speaking in tongues does not produce the results which I claim. But, the problem is not the process, it is the partnership. Praying in tongues on a regular basis will produce results, if you allow the relationship of His Spirit to flow into the troubled area of your life. Praying in tongues will energize you, there is no doubt. However, if you move to the basement when the winds come, refusing to deal with things in your life revealed by the wind of The Spirit, you will not have the fruit that should be in your life. You must give Him access to that area of your life for results to come.

Often, as you pray in the Spirit, He will talk to you. Listen intently. What is He saying to your spirit? Listen so you can hear the love song He is singing over you. Do you hear His loving reprimand? Is He telling you to turn loose of un-forgiveness? Or perhaps, like me, are you shocked when He zeroes in on specific sins in your life? Lean into His ability. Don't continue down the rut of compromise. Stop making excuses and allowances for your flesh. Grow up! There are places a believer doesn't go. Grow up! There are movies you shouldn't watch. Get your life on track…the track of discipleship that Christ laid - tracks that line up with the divine strategic principles of Scripture.

The crossing sign on the railroad track warns: Stop; Look; Listen. This is also great advice for every believer. Every day, stop and pray. Look in the Bible for direction. Listen to His still, small Voice. Listen, and then obey. How different your life would be if you established this simple process as a daily practice.

Diversities of Tongues

> Here is a list of some of the members that God has placed in the body of Christ: first are apostles, second are prophets, third are teachers, then those who do miracles, those who have the gift of healing, those who can help others, those who can get others to work together, those who speak in unknown languages. (1 Corinthians 12:28)

Dave Robeson explains that the diversities of tongues include four different kinds of tongues:
1. Tongues for personal edification;
2. Tongues for public worship which should be interpreted;
3. Tongues for intercession;
4. Tongues as a sign for the unbeliever.[46]

Understanding these differences helps us utilize His gifts properly and effectively.

Grafted In

In the agrarian culture of grape and olive cultivation, the picture of new birth, as illustrated by grafting, was readily understood. Romans 11:17 used this understanding to show the formation of a new tree by grafting a wild olive branch into a virile olive stock or root. Grafting is the process of taking a live branch and attaching it to a healthy root. The branch must be kept alive until the nourishment from its new host begins to flow into it. Successful grafting only requires that a vascular connection between two tissues is made. After a successful graft, the cutoff, wild, unfruitful, bitter olive branch shares - and is nourished by - the life and vitality from the root. The numerous benefits derived from grafting include: faster maturity; increased fruitfulness; higher quality of fruit; stronger, hardier, more disease- and temperature-tolerant trees; and, ease of propagation.[47]

Just as a successful graft produces a new tree, we are new creatures in Christ Jesus. "Therefore if any man be in Christ, he is a new creature..." (2 Corinthians 5:17 KJV) Redemption restores us to our rightful place, spiritually; then, relationship keeps vitality and life flowing through our being. The DNA or nature of the root flows into the branch. We cannot live a holy life without the nature of God flowing through us. As believers, we can do good things in our

---

[46] Dave Roberson *The Walk of the Spirit. The Walk of Power,* 1999.
[47] http://en.m.wikipedia.org/wiki/Grafting?wasRedirected=true

strength, but we cannot rise to the level God planned for us, which is beyond good. Grafting accomplishes that union. That vascular connection, which is essential for successful grafting, is accomplished as God's heart of love flows into a believer's life. We must keep our spirit open to continuously receive His grace, and keep His love flowing into our life. We must keep it open to receive all that God has for us. It will change us. It will make us more fruitful. It will make us like Christ. It will make us hardier, more mature, more resilient, and more resistant to sin.

Erik Weihenmayer

Let's look at a man who accomplished the impossible because he respected both processes and partnerships. His name is Erik Weihenmayer. He climbed to the summit of Mt Everest. As a matter of fact, he is one of only a 150 people who has ascended to the summit of the highest peaks on all seven continents; that is a remarkable feat for anyone, but especially extraordinary when you understand that Erik Weihenmayer is blind.

Impossible, you ask? How could he do it? Mountain climbing is both arduous and dangerous. The quest to summit Mt. Everest has claimed the lives of some of the world's best climbers. Erik was a true athlete and wanted to employ his abilities in his quest to climb the greatest mountains in the world. He refused to be carried and placed atop the summit, like spiking a football in the end zone. He wanted to actively participate in the venture. Before the climb, which would change his altitude, he had to change his attitude. He changed his thinking. He renounced the attitude that his lack, his inability to see, would ever again define who he was.[48]

The Bible is clear on the gravity of this subject. Be transformed - not by having a superstar preacher lay hands on you; not by fasting forty days; but, by renewing your mind. Change what you think.

---

[48]Top of the World, Erik Weihenmayerhttp://en.wikipedia.org/wiki/Erik_Weihenmayer http://www.touchthetop.com/about.htm (accessed June 1, 2011)

Partner - Wind

Embrace what God says about you. Grip the promise, not the problem. Grasp faith in God's ability, not your inability. Begin to fill your spirit with the promises of God.

Erik accomplished his goal because he understood and employed two basic mindsets: processes and partnerships; both of which made this exploit achievable.

First, Erik established deliberate, practical steps and procedures, which became regular habits that enabled him to reach his goal. His first baby steps for reaching the tip top of his first summit didn't seem to even be related to mountain climbing at all; he learned to read Braille and got his first guide dog. Numerous steps along the way prepared him for Mt. Everest. You can be confident that, as a blind, thirteen-year-old boy, he didn't begin with Mt. Everest.

Why do I mention the importance of processes? Processes are the things you do. Processes produce vital habits that move important things out of someday and into your daily schedule. I turn out the lights when I leave a room. I don't think about it; I just do it. Sometimes, I turn the lights out while Wayne is still in the room. I don't think about it; it's a habit. That habit won't make me a stronger Christian, but the habit of daily prayer will. I get up early and start my day with prayer. It is a habit I started as a little girl in the girls program at our church. Deliberately and strategically feeding my spirit will make me a stronger Christian. Here are some of the disciplines I have established in my personal life. For many years now, I use a reading plan to read through the Bible each year. By reading fifteen minutes a day with this plan, I can read through the Bible every year. I download books of the Bible that I am studying onto my MP3 player and listen to them again and again as I exercise or work around the house. I try to listen to at least one sermon every day. I listen to a variety of ministers online. Sometimes, I get interested in a sermon series and will listen to the same minister for several weeks. I deliberately plant the seed of the living Word of God into my spirit. If I notice that I am struggling in a particular area, I go to the medicine cabinet of God's Word and study that area. I study the Scriptures, looking for keys that will unlock victory in my life in that particular area. I write down the scriptures I find and pray them in my prayer time. I am convinced that prayer and Bible study are essential processes that keep my life on track.

The second enabling force that Erik utilized was the power of relationships and partnerships. The teachers that taught him and the team that climbed with him were vital elements of his personal success. Your partnership with Holy Spirit is vital to reaching your destiny. Your relationship with Him encourages, enriches, guides, and empowers your life. He's more than an abstract force that you plug into to get stuff. The partnership with the person of Holy Spirit is the most dynamic relationship that can be experienced by a human being.

Erik couldn't see where he was going, so he had to trust his partner. You're not always going to see everything. Your Partner, Holy Spirit, is not always going to give you the why or the how or the answer to that question that you may be waiting on. You must trust Him. He's there for you! He's got your back. Be confident that He is not going to throw you under the bus!

Too often, we treat him as if he were a weak, emaciated grandpa who we secretly hide in the back of the basement. News alert! He's not weak! He's not emaciated, and He shouldn't be a secret. His presence brings life and light. His presence brings joy. His presence brings the reality of Jesus. When Erik finally stood on the summit of Mt. Everest, amidst its grandeur, he felt triumphant in every fiber of his being. You can experience Holy Spirit's presence at a new level. Allow His boundaries to protect you and His promises to nourish you.

Prayer Partner

Powerful advocate, supporter, friend, prayer partner…did I say prayer partner? Can you imagine having a prayer partner who always knows God's perfect will for your life? Can you imagine a prayer partner who knows exactly what to pray and how to pray for every situation you need to pray about? Can you imagine a prayer partner who would pray with you any time you wanted to pray? Can you imagine a prayer partner who never prayed with fear or unbelief, or better still, never poisoned your mind with fear and unbelief? Can you imagine a prayer partner who always prayed the perfect will of God; a prayer partner who could bypass human reasoning to pray out the plan of God? Would you want to take that prayer partner with you when you prayed? Holy Spirit is exactly that kind of prayer partner. He knows the perfect will of God. Holy Spirit knows what to pray and how to pray. He wants to partner with you to help you pray.

Just as air partners with vocal cords and the larynx to produce syllables and words, Holy Spirit partners with you to help you pray. There is no area of our lives that we need God's help greater than in the exercise of prayer.

> Reader Harris said:
> Prayer is the supply-valve of power and blessing: The Christian's vital breath, the Christian's native air. Prayer, true prayer, is a mystery to those who are not filled with the Spirit. To some it is a labour, to others it is a form; but to those who know God and follow Him wholly it is A GLORIOUS PRIVILEGE. Prayer is God and man communing — through the Holy Ghost; prayer bridges the gulf between the finite and the Infinite, between earth and heaven. We shall never be the channels of blessing to men that God wants us to be, until we have learned to be the channels to Him and from Him that He desires.[49]

Samuel Chadwick talks about Spirit-empowered prayer:
> When the Church is run on the same lines as a circus, there may be crowds, but there is no Shekinah. That is why prayer is the test of faith and the secret of power. The Spirit of God travails in the prayer-life of the soul. Miracles are the direct work of His power, and without miracles the Church cannot live. The carnal can argue, but it is the Spirit that convicts.

---

[49] Harris, *When He is Come*, 59.

Pentecost Lost

> Education can civilize, but it is being born of the Spirit that saves. The energy of the flesh can run bazaars, organize amusements, and raise millions; but it is the presence of Holy Spirit that makes a Temple of the Living God. The root-trouble of the present distress is that the Church has more faith in the world and the flesh than in the Holy Ghost, and things will get no better till we get back to His realized presence and power. The breath of the four winds would turn death into life and dry bones into mighty armies, but it only comes by prayer.[50]

"And the Holy Spirit helps us in our distress. For, we don't even know what we should pray for, nor how we should pray. But the Holy Spirit prays for us with groanings that cannot be expressed in words." (Romans 8:26)

Samuel Chadwick states:
> He maketh intercession for us with groaning that cannot be uttered." None but the Spirit-filled know that kind of praying. It is the kind that wrought miracles in the Acts of the Apostles, and to this day prevails. It pleads the Name, enthrones the Name, and claims the Name. It prays in His will, presents His promise, and decrees in His Power. Prayer brings Pentecost, and Pentecost makes prayer omnipotent for all the will of God. The Spirit instructs and inspires prayer, gives intelligence and intensity to intercession, and brings reality and joy to communion with God. The Spirit-filled love to pray, and prayer that is in the Spirit must prevail.[51]

Holy Spirit partners with us to help us pray more effectively. I learned the importance of praying in tongues as a young mother. My children were in school, and I was praying at home. There were some things going on in our Sunday school class that troubled me. I was very uneasy about the situation, but understanding authority, I knew

---

[50] Samuel Chadwick, Way to Pentecost, 7.
[51] Ibid. 19.

it was not my place to say anything. Besides, maybe I was wrong, so I prayed. I prayed for my teacher and the situation that was going on, as best as I knew how. I prayed something like this, "God fill my teacher with wisdom. Show him how to handle this situation," and then I moved into praying in tongues. As I prayed in the Spirit, Holy Spirit reminded me of a few words from a verse. I searched for the verse using my concordance. This was the answer I was looking for. As I continued to pray, I felt an inner prompting to call my teacher and share the verse. So I called him.

Humbly, I shared how much I loved and appreciated this teacher and his wife; then, from a sincere heart of love and respect, I shared the verse with the teacher. I was shocked. His eyes seemed to pop open. He said, "You are right. That will never happen again." Holy Spirit worked on both ends of the situation. Holy Spirit had the answer all along. Praying in tongues brought revelation knowledge as He unlocked the answer in my spirit.

Here is a very important key. I didn't know the answer, but God did. As I prayed in the Spirit, the Holy Spirit was praying the perfect will of God. He helps our infirmities (the places where we are weak). He helps us pray with effectiveness, beyond what we could possible utter. He searches the mind of God to pray according to the will of God, which makes our prayer accurate, succinct, and effective, like an arrow going straight to the bull's eye.

Life's problems, issues, and controversies can be complex and convoluted. Often, I can see the perspective of both sides of an issue. But, what we need most is to see things through the lens of God's insight because He sees and knows the best and most viable solution. We can only access that solution by hearing His voice and allowing Him to lead us beyond raw knowledge to wisdom. He wants to talk to us. Praying in tongues opens our spirit, so we can recognize and hear His voice more easily.

Your Two Lips, Too!

Speaking is a partnership with air. The air moves over the vocal cords to produce sound that is adjusted by the larynx and shaped by the tongue, mouth, and nose to produce syllables that form words. A partnership between the air and your vocal organs make it possible for you to talk. Similarly, the alliance between you and Holy Spirit enables you to pray in the Spirit. It is a supernatural activity. You engage your natural ability to speak, and His supernatural ability supplies the words for you to speak.

> For if I pray in tongues, my spirit is praying, but I don't understand what I am saying. [15]Well then, what shall I do? I will do both. I will pray in the spirit, and I will pray in words I understand. I will sing in the spirit, and I will sing in words I understand. (1 Corinthians 14:14 -15)

Here, Paul, who is an intelligent and well educated man who wrote two thirds of the New Testament, explains: "I don't know what I'm saying when I pray in tongues." Why would he do it then? It was because he understood the importance and benefit of engaging precious Holy Spirit's help when He prayed. He understood he didn't need to understand because he wasn't talking to himself. He was talking to God in a language that bypassed human intellect to pray about the things God wanted him to pray about. Praying in an unknown tongue bypasses human selfishness and unbelief. It bypasses smallness and inadequacies to grasp the miraculous provision and wisdom that God has for the Church.

You can pray in tongues, or in the Spirit, using your prayer language any time you want. You don't have to have a special feeling or high emotional experience to pray in tongues. It is your private prayer language, which you can use like you would use your native language. I use my native language, which is English, to speak to other English-speaking people. I use my heavenly language when I am speaking to my heavenly Father. It is foolish to use it to communicate with unbelievers or anyone who doesn't understand it.

Partner - Wind

You and I were not given this language to bring confusion to people. When speaking to God, it is a powerful communication tool.

Guidelines

While Paul insists that we should not prohibit people from speaking in tongues, he outlines a boundary for its use in public worship. Paul explains clearly in 1 Corinthians 14:5: "I would like every one of you to speak in tongues, but I would rather have you prophesy. He who prophesies is greater than one who speaks in tongues, unless he interprets, so that the church may be edified." 1 Corinthians 13:1-6 guides us through the landmines of selfishness and pride that can sidetrack the most sincere believer. The focus of ministry in church must be to comfort, edify, and exhort the church. It is not to distract, draw attention to one's self, or dazzle someone with your spirituality. All efforts to minister should flow out of selfless, compassionate love.

> Let love be your highest goal, but also desire the special abilities the Spirit gives, especially the gift of prophecy. ^{2} For if your gift is the ability to speak in tongues, you will be talking to God but not to people, since they won't be able to understand you. You will be speaking by the power of the Spirit, but it will all be mysterious. ^{3}But one who prophesies is helping others grow in the Lord, encouraging and comforting them. ^{4}A person who speaks in tongues is strengthened personally in the Lord, but one who speaks a word of prophecy strengthens the entire church. ^{5}I wish you all had the gift of speaking in tongues, but even more I wish you were all able to prophesy. For prophecy is a greater and more useful gift than speaking in tongues, unless someone interprets what you are saying so that the whole church can get some good out of it. ^{18}I thank God that I speak in tongues more than all of you. ^{19}But in a church meeting I would much rather speak five understandable words that will help others than ten thousand words in an unknown language.
>
> --1 Corinthians 14:1-5, 18-19

Pentecost Lost

Don't forget these guidelines are written with the understanding that we should speak in tongues; yet, when in church, speak within the boundaries of common sense and etiquette that comes with a heart of consideration and concern for others first. Paul is guiding us to use the right tool for the task. You don't use a screw driver to drive a nail. There's a tool for edifying ourselves and a different tool for edifying the church. When edifying our own self, we pray in tongues. When edifying the church, we either prophesy or employ the gift of tongues with interpretation.

While I believe speaking in tongues should NOT be relegated to a dark corner of the church, as if we were ashamed of Holy Spirit, I believe we must subject the operation of this manifestation to mature wisdom and love. It is not my intention to bog us down with details of etiquette that should envelope this manifestation, yet I do want to give an example that illustrates appropriate timing of its use.

As I have engaged in teacher training over the years, I have been in all the major denominations extending beyond the Pentecostal arenas. The leader of an inter-denominational conference was encouraged to meet for united prayer over the conference and financial woes that the organization was facing. We gathered in a circle, and one by one, we prayed. One lady in the group had just experienced a time of refreshing and renewal in her life. She was excited about the things that God was doing in her life, but that doesn't excuse the events that followed. When it came her turn to pray, she prayed robustly in tongues. There was no interpretation, and very few in the room understood what was happening. Then, she dramatically announced that if the people did not repent, God would write Ichabod over the organization. You could feel the air being sucked out of the room. When people didn't respond as she felt they should, she left the room, packed her things, and went home. Because the message was not tempered with love or delivered in a spirit of compassion and humility, it caused damage instead of bringing life to a meeting that was already struggling. I know that there are times for tough messages to be delivered, but she was moving outside her realm of authority and compassion. That is never a good thing.

Public praying in tongues should fit within the boundaries and guidelines of Scripture without being banned from church. Often, before I give an altar call, I will ask people to bow their heads. I explain that I need God's help and direction for this time of response. I might begin like this: "So, for just a few minutes, let's quiet our spirits and listen to God. If you have received Holy Spirit and want to join me, I am going to pray in my prayer language. It is a language God gives believers to pray more efficiently. As I pray in the spirit, I listen for direction and insight. Often, the gifts of the Spirit will begin to operate, as I make His Spirit a priority."

Many times, before I lay hands on people to pray for them, I will quiet my spirit and pray in tongues. As I pray in the Spirit over those people, I believe Holy Spirit is allowing me to pray God's perfect will over them. Then, when I begin to pray in English, my prayer is very focused and full of revelation knowledge, often prophetic in nature. I find my prayer for a person in English is more strategic when I pray in tongues first.

Inhale, Exhale

Breathing requires both inhaling and exhaling! Prayer requires both. Breathe in life, and breathe out worship. Not only does Holy Spirit help you ask more effectively, He also helps you worship more deeply. Holy Spirit gives us a holy vocabulary to express your love and to worship God in a way that He enjoys. Mike Adkins sings a beautiful, anointed worship song called, "Adoration." He worships with words that exalt the name and goodness of God, and then he ends by singing in tongues. It is a powerful and inspiring song. In 1 Cor. 14:15, Paul said, "I will sing with the spirit, and I will sing with the understanding also."

It was a tropical paradise. I slowed my pace to enjoy the lush plants, glorious sunshine, and perfect temperature. The water seemed

Pentecost Lost

to be playing "Hide and Go Seek" as it splashed my feet and then ran away. It was peaceful and almost quiet, except for the squawk of gulls and the roar of crashing waves; yet, somehow, their sounds added to the ambiance instead of disturbing it. Night came quickly and the sun kissed the horizon goodnight with a glorious display of vibrant colors. I was tired by the time I crawled in bed, so sleep came almost instantly.

Noises typically don't awaken me, but this shrill sound was so loud, I awoke, alarmed. When I slid open the sliding glass door that led to the balcony, the piercing sound flooded the room. I thought the shrill, cyclical sound was a fire alarm. Frightened, I dialed the front desk and waited impatiently for the attendant to answer the phone.

"Is there a fire alarm going off in the hotel somewhere?" I asked without a greeting.

Unruffled, she answered with a question, "Is there an alarm going off in your room?"

"No. But it sounds as if one is going off somewhere on the grounds."

"We don't have an alarm going off anywhere," she assured me.

"Then what is that loud noise?" I continued.

"What loud noise?"

I apologized for the interruption and hung up the phone. "What loud noise? You've got to be kidding me!" I said to myself. Where was that sound coming from?

The shrill, alarming sound continued night after night, and so did my search for the source of the sound. No one seemed to hear it, much less know what it was.

Finally, on the way to my room one night, I found it. I couldn't believe my eyes. That loud, cyclical sound was coming from a chorus of tiny, one-inch frogs.

One inch! Can you believe that? Those frogs were no longer than the length from the tip of my finger to the first joint. I crept up on one and watched his entire body fill with air as he bellowed out that shrill, irritating noise. Another frog answered the first, then a third frog, and it continued until it made its way back to the first little racket maker. I think a one-inch frog is way too little to make that big of a noise, but size didn't stop those frogs.

That should be the mindset of a believer. You should not allow size, age, situations, lack, fear, or anything else to limit or stop your praise. Scripture tells us in Psalms 150:6: "Let everything that lives sing praises to the LORD! Praise the LORD!"

You're not too busy, too old, nor too needy to praise the Lord, but you could be too lazy or too selfish. Your voice of praise penetrates heaven. The presence of God moves toward you when you praise Him. "But thou art holy, O thou that inhabitest the praises of Israel." (Psalms 22:3 KJV)

> The leading priests and the teachers of religious law saw these wonderful miracles and heard even the little children in the Temple shouting, "Praise God for the Son of David." But they were indignant [16]and asked Jesus, "Do you hear what these children are saying?" "Yes," Jesus replied. "Haven't you ever read the Scriptures? For they say, 'You have taught children and infants to give you praise." (Matthew 21:15-16)

Your praise is powerful. It silences the enemy and the voice of the avenger. "You have taught children and nursing infants to give you praise. They silence your enemies who were seeking revenge." (Psalms 8:2)

Do more than only talk about the power of praise! Praise Him right now, aloud if you are not in a public place. It may feel awkward if you've never done it before. Take another step; raise your hands like a baby reaching for its mama, and then express your love to Him in your words or words you borrow from the Psalms.

Psalms gives us proper decorum into the presence of the King of Kings with, "Enter into his gates with thanksgiving and into His courts with praise." (Psalm 100:4) Praise is heaven's protocol to enter God's presence. Start your prayer time with thanksgiving and praise. Thanksgiving is giving thanks for things He has done. He is the source and giver of every good thing in your life. Praise goes beyond thankfulness to recognize and extol His nature and distinguishing attributes. Praise is the entrance to a more intimate level of God's presence.

Wind Talkers

The sunrise kissed away the darkness to display a magnificent lush paradise. Sunlight sparkled on the waves like diamonds on a wealthy oil baron's finger. Palm fronds swayed in the gentle breezes coming off the Pacific Ocean. This tropical delight was Oahu, Hawaii. It was 7:47 on a sleepy, Sunday morning. The date was December 7, 1941. World War II had been raging between France, the British Commonwealth, and Germany since September 1939. As the plague of war advanced, other nations joined the warfare. Military strategists stockpiled Pearl Harbor with a vast arsenal of bombers, submarines, and battleships that were outfitted with the earth's most advanced technologies. The world was in turmoil, but the United States was not at war, so Pearl Harbor was quiet and peaceful. This pearl of the Pacific was considered unconquerable, invisible, and even untouchable.

At 7:48 a.m., Pacific Time, that peace was obliterated, literally blown to smithereens, when Japan attacked Pearl Harbor. Slow, vulnerable, torpedo bombers led the first wave, taking advantage of the first moments of surprise by attacking the most important targets: the battleships first, and then dive bombers attacked U.S. air bases across Oahu. Soldiers aboard U.S. ships awoke to the screams of bombs exploding. Alarms and gunfire sent bleary-eyed men dashing to their stations, pulling on their clothes as they ran. The headquarters of Patrol Wing Two screamed the first message, "Air raid Pearl Harbor. This is not a drill." Despite their vast arsenal, they were rendered totally defenseless. In the confusion that followed, ammunition and guns locked in cabinets could not be accessed. Aircraft parked wingtip to wingtip to deter sabotage made airborne resistance almost impossible. Huge guns and powerful defense weapons were unmanned or damaged, drastically limiting their ability to defend themselves.

This unprovoked, surprise attack catapulted America into World War II. On December 8, President Roosevelt asked the Congress to declare war on Japan. Congress voted unanimously to go to war.

As illustrated by Japan's surprise attack at Pearl Harbor, America would need a strong, secret strategy to assure military success. That stratagem required expedient transmission and utmost secrecy. Military forces expected their messages to be intercepted for several reasons. American troops were especially vulnerable because many Japanese military leaders had graduated from American Universities. These Japanese commanders spoke and understood English as well as any of the radio operators broadcasting messages to troops in the battlefield. Their effort to shroud their battle plans in secret code failed repeatedly.

In 1942, Philip Johnston read a newspaper article describing efforts to devise a new secret code using Native American languages. Native American languages had been used successfully as code in World War I. Because this fact was common knowledge, both Japan and Germany had sent students to learn the languages and cultures of the Cherokee, Choctaw, and Comanche. Because this reality was widely acknowledged, many military strategists were apprehensive, even opposed to the development of a new code based on a Native American language.

Johnston was intrigued. As a missionary kid, he had grown up among the Navajo. He understood the complexity of their language. Johnston wrote letters to military leaders asserting that the Navajo language could be utilized in a new code, and that he was confident it could not be broken. The Navajo language seemed to be the perfect option for two major reasons: it is not a written language, and it had been confined to only a few people outside their tribe. Despite reservations, the U.S. Marine Corps decided to give Johnston's idea a try. Phillip Johnston and twenty-nine Navajo recruits began to develop a new code. The Marine Corps took the code to the next level and made it virtually unbreakable by further encoding the language with word substitution. During the course of the war, about four hundred Navajos participated in the code talker program.

Pentecost Lost

These Wind Talkers, the name given to these Navajo field radio operators, relayed orders, vital strategies, and messages from headquarters in their native language. Then, Navajo Wind Talkers on the other end decoded the messages to align troops, airplanes, and battleships accordingly. The Navajo Code was never broken. By speaking and interpreting this secret code, the Wind Talkers facilitated victory after victory until the war was won. The Wind Talkers are credited with saving thousands of lives and shortening the war by at least two years.

I am convinced your prayer language is a secret code, which the enemy, satan, and all his cronies can't understand. I believe there is deliberate, strategic reasoning behind God giving a believer the ability to pray words they do not understand. "And pray in the Spirit on all occasions with all kinds of prayers and requests. With this in mind, be alert and always keep on praying for all the saints." (Ephesians 6:18 NIV)

Praying in the Spirit, or praying in tongues, is a powerful, prayer weapon. Spirit filled believers, similar in function to the Navajo Wind Talkers, are transmitting secret codes we don't understand. The funny sounding words or syllables we speak transmit needs, requests, and worship to God. We are praying the will of God. We are in a battle, and we must use the strategic weapons we have been given, if we want to win and help others win.

There are three primary reasons you should pray in your prayer language regularly.

1. You are praying God's perfect will when you pray in tongues. "And the Holy Spirit helps us in our distress. For we don't even know what we should pray for, nor how we should pray. But the Holy Spirit prays for us with groanings that cannot be expressed in words. ^{27}And the Father who knows all hearts knows what the Spirit is saying, for the Spirit pleads for us believers in harmony with God's own will." (Romans 8:26, 27)

It would probably surprise us to realize how much of our prayer time revolves around ourselves. Give me. Help me. Me! Me! Me! We all pray more selfish prayers than we should, but when we pray in the

Spirit, our prayer is free from carnal, selfish desires and perspectives. Untangled, now we can pray about the things that are important to God.

2. Because you are praying without engaging your reasoning, your mind cannot attack your prayer with unbelief and fear. Have you ever prayed arduously and fervently for something, but the entire time you prayed you struggled with unbelief and fear? Or, have you ever prayed with a gnawing skepticism that no matter how long or how hard you prayed, you would never receive your request? I have. That unbelief will strip prayer victories right out of your life, like a linebacker strips the ball from the arms of a running back.

When you pray in the Spirit, your mind isn't saying, "That's BIG! You can't ask God for that! You're not good enough or spiritual enough or on and on the thoughts go… That will never happen, or that is a horrible disease; I can't ask God to heal that disease." No, your mind is not praying. His Spirit is praying beyond your grasp, all the way to the perfect will of God.

3. Praying in the Spirit builds spiritual muscles, making you stronger, just like exercise builds physical muscles. "But you, dear friends, build yourselves up in your most holy faith and pray in Holy Spirit." (Jude 1:20 NIV)

I cannot conclude my story of the conquests of World War II, facilitated by the Wind Talkers, without mentioning one major problem this unit faced. The military could not recruit sufficient numbers of Wind Talkers; there just weren't enough of them.

I believe God's dispatch headline reads something like this: "Wind Talkers Needed!" God is looking for boys and girls and men and women who will pray in their heavenly language, worship God in their prayer language, and intercede in their prayer language, bombarding heaven until God's will invades this planet. Would things be different in our communities if the bulletin board in our local church read, "Wind Talkers Meet this Saturday" instead of only "Ball Players Meet this Saturday"? Seize the opportunity to participate in bringing divine intervention to our culture by praying in tongues.

Pentecost Lost

I can see the headlines, "Wind Talkers Help Win the War!" There was never a headline like that, because the mission was classified as secret. No one, not even the families of the Wind Talkers, knew the important contribution these Navajo soldiers were making to win the war. They couldn't brag. They couldn't even mention it.

I must warn you, if you become a Holy Spirit-empowered Wind Talker, no one is going to brag on you. No one is going to even know how hard you have prayed, or how you have sacrificed your time, because Wind Talkers operate from their secret place. Your secret place can be anywhere: your bedroom at home, or going down the road riding your bike, or behind the vacuum cleaner in your den. Wind Talkers don't seek a "show place;" they seek a "low place," because they understand their voice is a weapon, encased in the power of Holy Spirit to entreat God's intervention. People may never acknowledge your position in the battle, but God will. God rewards openly what He sees happening in secret.

But, they were rewarded many years later. After the secret mission of the Navajo Wind Talkers was declassified in 1968, their function was finally recognized and rewarded. All twenty-nine original Wind Talkers were awarded the Congressional Medal of Honor.

When you are in your secret place praying in tongues, with satan screaming in your ear, "You're wasting your time; you don't have time to pray; you're not even praying," please tell him to hush - and don't stop praying!

Let me encourage you, - please keep on praying. Remember, one day you will be brought into the presence of the King of Kings and Lord of Lords, then He'll reward you with a reward so amazing there are no words to describe it.

I am convinced there has to be a reason that the enemy tries to push this gift of speaking in tongues into a dark corner and cloak it with a huge and menacing danger sign. Clearly, we see scripture after scripture where Paul validates the use of praying in tongues, yet there remains great controversy or dubious apathy in the church; both of which cause its neglect. Satan's strategy to stop the church seems intensified in regards to speaking in tongues. While I understand

Pentecostals have given skeptics reason to cringe and even recoil on occasions, there seems to be a diabolical strategy in place to stop people from praying in tongues. I am convinced it is because satan is threatened by this powerful and effective weapon and is determined to prevent its use. It is time to believe what satan already knows: praying in tongues is a viable, powerful weapon that can be used to stop the strategies of hell. When we sincerely believe it is a strategic weapon, we will pray in tongues on a regular and consistent basis.

Listen!

> William Robinson Clark states:
> Many lessons of unspeakable value have been communicated to the Church during the ages that have gone by; and those who have ears to hear may listen and learn still from the oracles of the living God interpreted by the Spirit of Truth. Yea, we are sure the time will never come when the Voice of the Spirit shall be silent and the members of Christ shall have no more to learn concerning the mysteries of the Kingdom.[52]

The role of paraclete during your prayer time is more than helping you utter powerful prayers. He is not a silent partner; He has a voice, and He wants to speak into your life. Creation only begins to display His boundless creativity and limitless ability. When you ask for wisdom, expect Him to reveal it to you. I'm not inferring it will be instantaneous, but He will guide you. Pay attention to the strong thoughts or impressions that come to you as you are praying in the Spirit. Write them down. Ask for clarity and understanding.

While praying in tongues one day, I began to notice that I was repeating a word-- Lodebar. When I finished praying, I searched my *Strong's Concordance* to see if it was a word in the Bible. (You can use the *Strong's Concordance* online at crossway.com) My search took me to the story of Mephibosheth, who was hiding in Lodebar and fearful that King David was going to kill him. Lodebar means "barren place."

---

[52]Clark, *The Paraclete*, 62.

Pentecost Lost

When King David found Mephibosheth, instead of killing him, he brought him to live in the palace and eat at the king's table[53]. Mephibosheth was crippled from a fall as a child.[54] But, the tablecloth that covered the table covered Mephibosheth's broken legs.

As I reread that story, precious Holy Spirit spoke to my heart: "I have taken you from a barren place to sit at my table. I am covering the places where you have been broken in the past with the table cloth of my grace and sufficiency." It was a powerful revelation from which I continue to draw strength. I would have missed that powerful revelation if I had not taken the time to listen and meditate on what Holy Spirit was saying.

Often, as I pray in tongues, I get ideas for my writing projects or I hear solutions to problems. Also, prayer needs are brought to my mind. Even the prayers I pray with my understanding are different. I hear myself praying for things in a way that I've never even considered before. I seem to have a fresh awareness that is beyond my personality. My constant prayer is: "Lord, help me to see this person or this situation through the lens of your love and insight." I am seeing that take place more frequently as I pray in the Spirit.

---

[53] 2 Samuel 9
[54] 2 Samuel 4:4

Partner - Wind

Think about it:
___

DUI: Dwell Under the Influence

Dear God, What do you want me to take away from this chapter?

Pray in tongues daily, not just this week. Make praying in tongues a lifestyle.

Chapter Five

Passion- Fire

I'm Cold!

It was the worst ice storm in years. Tree limbs, heavy with ice, snapped and crashed to the ground, bringing power lines down with them. The broken lines brought widespread power outages, leaving hundreds of shivering people wearing sweaters and heavy coats inside their homes. Work crews scrambled to restore power to the areas with the largest population first, leaving rural communities with fewer homes last on the list.

Without power, the elderly couple tried to keep warm inside their desolate, mountain home. The cold wind howled outside. It was almost as cold inside as it was outside, since their hundred-plus-year-old farmhouse didn't have any insulation. Ma pulled another blanket out of the closet and headed back to the family room. Pa rubbed his hands together briskly and stomped across the room to get warm blood flowing to his feet. Both Ma and Pa saw it at the same time. Pa laughed and Ma gasped, "The fireplace! Does that thing still work?"

Pa nodded and responded as he turned to go outside, "Yes, it does!"

It hadn't been used in years. It was almost hidden. The mantel was cluttered with "stuff," and the fireplace screen was barely visible behind the junk piled in front. Without another word, Ma started cleaning away the hearth and removing the screen while Pa gathered wood from the old wood stack behind the shed outback. She opened the flue and moved to one side as Pa piled tinder in the fireplace opening and struck a match. He watched the fire start, and when it was blazing, he added kindling (or small twigs) while Ma blew gently until the twigs caught fire. So he didn't smother the fire, Pa deliberately and watchfully added medium and then larger pieces of wood until a hot fire roared in the fireplace. It didn't take long until the room was warm, and they both were peeling off their coats. The fireplace had been there all along, but they weren't warmed by it until a fire was lit.

It breaks my heart to say this, but this is a picture of too many church goers. They have a fireplace, a place reserved for a fire, but there is no fire in their heart.

> What an extraordinary thing this must be for angels and devils to see! Men and women created by God, redeemed by Christ, living on this earth, which is flying through space at the rate of a thousand miles a minute; living, they do not know why; dying, they do not know when; certain to have to stand before the Bar of God; and yet hesitating to claim Holy Spirit, the great Gift whom God their Creator offers them, and without whom they cannot please Him![55]

We need the fire of Holy Spirit burning on the altar of our heart as much as the first church needed it.

Yuck! It's Luke...

I love coffee. The explosion of Starbuck's popularity attests to the fact that I am not alone; America loves coffee. While I prefer it strong and black, I'll drink it any way you serve it. I enjoy it plain or flavored, iced or screaming hot. I enjoy coffee at any hour of the day. But, as much as I love coffee, I hate lukewarm coffee. I won't drink it lukewarm. I think of Revelation 3:16 every time I get a sip of coffee that has cooled to lukewarm.

God vehemently expressed His disapproval of lukewarm people with a vivid metaphor: "So then because thou art lukewarm, and

---

[55] Harris, *When He is Come*, 16.

Pentecost Lost

neither cold nor hot, I will spew thee out of my mouth." (Revelation 3:16 KJV)

Your cup of coffee will get lukewarm if it sits idle too long. As long as the cup is emptied and then refilled from a hot source, its contents will be hot. The process of repeated filling and emptying is heaven's strategy for every believer: be filled with God's grace and emptied out in ministry to others.

Coffee will also become lukewarm if you mix a little hot into a cup of cold. Metaphorically, this is a picture of a believer trying to have a little bit of God and a little bit of the world, which results in a disgusting mix. It is disgusting to the world, and it is displeasing to God for a church or a believer to be lukewarm. The world laughs at the phoniness they see in the church world. God warns the lukewarm church that they are deceived. They see themselves as rich, but He warns them that they are destitute. God, open our eyes to see our need. Father, help us not to sit naked when you have clean garments to clothe us. God, ignite our hearts with passion, so we will love you too much to live our lives removed from the fire.

Fire

Fire represented the presence of God. In Hebrews 12:29, we read: "For our God is a consuming fire." Many significant God encounters recorded in the Bible were marked with fire, like modern celebrations are marked with fireworks. Fiery manifestations make you stop and look.

Moses saw a burning bush in the wilderness and moved closer to solve the mystery.[56] When he did, he encountered God. An ominous, supernatural fire rumbled and smoked on Mt. Sinai, and the voice of God spoke to the Israelites on the first Pentecost.[57] A pillar of fire warmed the Israelites in the wilderness at night when the temperature dropped drastically.[58] The fire of the lamp stand in the

---

[56] Exodus 3:3
[57] Exodus 19:18
[58] Exodus 13:21

Passion - Fire

Holy Place was to burn perpetually.[59] God answered Elijah's prayer with fire from heaven.[60]

John answered their questions by saying, "I baptize with water; but someone is coming soon who is greater than I am -- so much greater that I am not even worthy to be his slave. He will baptize you with the Holy Spirit and with fire." (Luke 3:16) And He did. Again, God demonstrated His presence one more time with fire on the day of Pentecost. Tongues of fire sat on each of the 120 believers who were gathered. Why fire? Why tongues of fire? God was deliberate in His strategy. Fire is a clue that unlocks the mystery of one aspect of the work of Holy Spirit in believers.

Think about the last time you snuggled around a blazing fire. Maybe it was cold and snowy outside, or maybe it was a starlit night at camp. What did you see? What did you hear? Do you remember how you felt? I love the gentle glow and the ambiance of a fire; the romantic, peaceful, cozy feeling warms me inside as much as outside. Yet, the benefits of a fire far exceeds ambiance. Industry requires it for manufacturing goods and refining precious metals. Car engines propel us along roadways burning fuel. Our sophisticated, modern culture continues to benefit from fire.

But, why did God use fire at Pentecost? First, fire was a recognized precedent or symbol for the presence of God. Anyone who knew Jewish history understood the significance of fire. They readily understood fire was essential for life. It was the only method to cook their food and warm their homes. God was conveying a picture that spoke a thousand words to this culture and ours, as seen through the lens of their customs, "You've got to have me. I am essential. My presence brings abundant life."

Their homes were illuminated by the flame of a candle or a lamp. The fire of Pentecost illuminates the soul of the believer; it enlightens the heart to understand the Bible, so the meaning is clear and its message is relevant. The light of Holy Spirit shatters the barrier of

---

[59]Leviticus 6:13
[60] 1 Kings 18:17-46

humanistic intellect to help a believer understand and value what is genuinely valuable. Holy Spirit lights up the face of Jesus for you to see. Allow Holy Spirit to add meaning to the instructions and principles of Scripture. Practice savoring the Scriptures, like you would a really good-quality, decadent chocolate.

This illumination of wisdom is not relegated to the spiritual realm alone. His wisdom should flow into every sphere of your life. "Knowledge is power" and "It's who you know that counts" are two idioms that find their realization in Jesus. There are steps to success, but the secret to success is discovering the right steps. Knowledge is the small sign in tiny letters that is hidden on the pathway for you to find. Because of who you know, you can ask Him for guidance and Divine favor. I wish His guidance was broader and more specific, but generally, it is only given a baby step at a time. We need both knowledge and the wisdom to apply that knowledge. "Study to shew thyself approved unto God, a workman that needeth not to be ashamed, rightly dividing the word of truth." (2 Timothy 2:15 KJV) That was Paul's instruction to Timothy. To that practical and vital advice I add: use a light - or better yet - The Light, when you study. I depend on His favor to open the right door with the same tenacity I depend on His illumination to bring clarity and knowledge that is needed for excellence in every corner of my life.

Holy Spirit's presence will also illuminate hidden sin. I live in Florida where we enjoy lots of rain and magnificent oak trees, both of which promote the proliferation of cockroaches. Our cockroaches, or palmetto bugs as some call them, are nothing like the tiny variety that northern housewives screech over. These fellows are big! And when you step on one, they give off a ghastly, horrific stench. Most of the time, I'm not even aware that roaches are nearby, but if I have to run outside at night, I get a quick reminder. As soon as I flip on the light to dart outside, I hear movement, which startles me every time. It is palmetto bugs scrambling for a hiding place in the leaves. Holy Spirit wants to illuminate your sin, so you are not ravaged by its consequences.

Passion - Fire

I was converted when I was four years old. I have sincerely and earnestly followed Christ all these years. I try to be a good Christian, yet I have found as I pray in tongues daily, my desire to be more like Christ deepens. In that process, He shows me things that are displeasing to Him. I discover that I'm not nearly as good as I would like to think I am. I can sugar coat it with excuses, or I can accept the truth. When His light shines, there's always a roach or two that runs out. I don't like to see my faults. I much prefer to hear Him express His love, so my first response is to be coy or make excuses. But, if I continue praying in tongues regularly, the gentle voice prompts me to deal with my sin. If I don't deal with it, guilt can begin to fester. I need to pause here to clarify. There is a huge difference between guilt and conviction. Conviction leads to change and action. Guilt demoralizes and debilitates. Guilt buries you in hopelessness.

When Holy Spirit brings illumination and conviction, you are forced to make a choice: ignore or repent. You can ignore it and stop praying in tongues. It is much easier to just ignore the conviction if you just stop praying in tongues. Easier! Perhaps...sometimes, but never better. (I have discovered that, if people continue to ignore conviction, they will quit praying in tongues regularly. They'll get too busy, or whatever excuse they decide to use, but they'll find a reason to quit.) Hopefully, you will pay attention to what Holy Spirit is revealing to you. You'll draw closer to the fire, so it consumes wrong desires and energizes you to live out loud what He says in secret. You can be confident the work of Holy Spirit doesn't stop with exposing sin. He wants to eradicate it. When you see sin, repent - sincerely repent - and turn from the sin. Precious Holy Spirit will give you the ability to defeat that sin in your life.

Another picture found in the Old Testament is a refiner's fire. A refiner heats precious metals to a liquid state, where impurities rise to the surface and the watchful refiner skims them off. Most of us want the power of Holy Spirit, but we prefer to exempt, or excuse, ourselves from the fire that purifies. We must allow Holy Spirit to purify us, sanitizing even our thoughts and emotions. We must allow His blaze to incinerate any and every sin that robs us of faith and

Pentecost Lost

faithfulness. Embrace the prayer of the Psalmist, "Search me, O God, and know my heart..." (Psalms 139:23) Let's allow Him to cremate the saplings that grow out of our carnal nature. As we throw the brambles of sin onto the fire of surrender, they emblazon us with the purposes of God, so our life is more meaningful and purposeful.

> Reader Harris states:
> Obey the light you have. Say "yes" to God at every point. If your all is on the altar it will be easy to say "yes" and to mean it. Obey the light He gives in everything. Some things, perhaps not sinful, may have to be given up; others will be undertaken at His command. Live in chastity of soul; let the light into the realm of your affections. Live in chastity of body; let the light in upon your habits. Live in chastity of mind; let the light illumine your thoughts.[61]

A fire warns us and warms us; don't miss the fire of Holy Spirit that warms our hearts with compassion. He melts our indifference. The icicles of selfishness and pride melt into a puddle of compassion in the presence of Holy Spirit fire. The fire of God ignites our passion, or fervent love, for God and everything connected with God. As this passion flows out of you, I think you'll be astonished that love, God's kind of love, doesn't even resemble the picture the world has painted of love.

The fire of Pentecost sat on each of them. Pentecost was not a fireplace experience; it was not a pilgrimage to a place to be warmed and then return to normal life again. The tongues of fire didn't rest on a building, which could be turned into a shrine. Instead, it rested on each individual, indicating that Holy Spirit would not fill a place; instead, He filled individual believers. Pentecost was a personal experience, with a personal fire burning on the altar of their heart.

I love the words of William Robinson Clark that describe the fire of Holy Spirit:

---

[61] Harris, *When He is Come*, 83.

"Our God is a consuming fire," Rom. viii. 9 and God is here; for it is God Himself who now comes to dwell with men, to remove the coldness of selfishness and death, and to kindle men to life and love, to drive away the darkness of nature and of sin, and to shed abroad the light of grace and holiness; to purify men from evil, to raise them up from all that is low, and earthly, and base. It was the new Law of the Church of God, given by fire, as the ancient Law had been given, but not amid thunder and lightning, but with the gentle light of love, and with a sound as of the rushing of a mighty wind, which spoke of the presence of an irresistible power.

We might here note one significant feature in this supernatural manifestation. The tongue of fire rested upon each one of the disciples present. There was not one exempted from the gift and the blessing. Now, this gift has not been withdrawn from the Church. The Paraclete, the Blessed Spirit of God, was given that He might abide with us forever; and He now dwells in the mystical Body of Christ that He may impart life to all its members and infuse the Spirit of love into their hearts and lives. They that are Christ's are still and ever under the guidance of this Spirit…[62]

Fire Fighters or Fire Lighters

In Leviticus 24:2, God commanded the priest to keep the lamps in the tabernacle burning continually…but the priests in Acts 5:18-42 looked more like fire fighters than fire lighters. Why didn't they grasp what God was doing?

Astonishing acts were happening in the book of Acts. Amazing miracles, like those Jesus performed, were bringing the crowds into Jerusalem. Large numbers of men and women believed Jesus and received Him as their Messiah. People had such great faith that they brought their sick from far away and laid them along the street, expecting them to be healed from a mere touch of Peter's shadow. (Acts 5:15) People tormented by evil spirits were set free. Blind eyes

---

[62]Clark, *The Paraclete,* 117.

Pentecost Lost

were opened. People received the infilling of Holy Spirit. I can only imagine the celebration that must have followed God's handiwork.

But, the priests were not celebrating.[63] They were fuming! Resentful and jealous, these religious leaders plotted to extinguish the fire before it spread. But, wait a minute. This was God's fire; a fire extinguisher wasn't needed. They should have been the first to understand the revelation of God's mystery. However, it seemed they were more interested in keeping their political power than pleasing God. They felt threatened by Jesus' success. Their fears blinded their faith, which kept them from recognizing their promised Savior. The priests used their political power to throw the apostles in jail, reasoning that it would douse the believer's enthusiasm and quiet the chatter about Jesus being God's Son.

Prison bars held the apostles for a while, but at midnight, they had a heavenly visitor. An angel of the Lord opened the doors for them and told them to get busy preaching the gospel again. Early the next morning, the apostles obeyed God by returning to the synagogue to preach the good news of Jesus Christ to the people.

When the priests sent for the imprisoned apostles, they discovered the guards were stationed at their posts outside locked doors, but the apostles were missing. A frantic informant brought more bad news, "Did you know those preachers you arrested are teaching in the synagogue?"

What a miracle! Can you imagine something like that happening to you? Walking out of locked doors isn't a cute fairy tale told to tickle your ears.

This miracle is the reality of God's power in response to believers' prayers. It is tragic that the religious leaders didn't recognize that they were seeing God's redemption story being unfolded before their eyes. Their religious traditions and carnality blinded them from the truth of Jesus.

This should be a warning to every believer. Even religious leaders can be deceived and misled. All of us are clay pots. We must also be

---

[63] Acts 5:18-42

Passion - Fire

constantly aware that the work of the flesh is a fire extinguisher. The priests missed Jesus, and the modern Church is missing the infilling of Holy Spirit. The infilling of Holy Spirit is not automatic. He has been sent into the world, but we must ask and believe to receive Him.

Again, the apostles were brought before the priest. "Didn't we tell you not to preach about Jesus?"

They answered, "We have to obey God and not man." Their answer surged into a sermon about Jesus. They had already slept behind bars. They had experienced prison brutality personally. These brave men were the same men who Jesus found frightened and secreted behind locked doors after His resurrection. What happened? The fire of Holy Spirit lit a brazen passion that enabled them to face their accusers. Jesus was more precious to them than their life. That's what the fire of passion does in a believer.

"When you set yourself on fire, people love to come and see you burn."— John Wesley.

Passion

Passion is a powerful and compelling emotion. It is also used as a noun to describe "the sufferings of Christ on the cross or His suffering subsequent to the Last Supper."[64] Without minimizing His suffering, I believe Christ's passion far exceeds His suffering. His love for us was and continues to be passionate. His love is active, full of compassion and forgiveness. His love is not generic but focused to kiss the heart of the individual. His love is visionary and insightful, seeing past our actions and inconsistencies to our need. His passion purchased and presented what no one else could ever propose — redemption: full and free. His passion painted redemption on the canvas of time with bold strokes of forgiveness, grace, and acceptance. It transforms the recipient, releasing talents and kindness, and it transcends time without losing its potency. Its latent power is released in the heart of

---

[64]"passion" *Dictionary.com Unabridged*. Random House, Inc. 02 Sep. 2010. <Dictionary.com http://dictionary.reference.com/browse/passion>.

anyone who will receive Him. Redemption prepared a dwelling place in the heart of a believer for the indwelling of Holy Spirit that we might be filled. And as the scripture suggests, we might keep being filled, allowing the overflow of His presence to flow thorough us and out to humanity.

The early church was born in the fire of Holy Spirit--a fire of passion. It was not a reckless, selfish wildfire, but a healthy robust passion. They experienced the same kind of passion exemplified by the apostles and believers through the years that have "loved not their lives to the death."[65] They experienced the same kind of passion Christ modeled for us in both His life and death through the power of Holy Spirit: passion that exhilarated their emotions and their lifestyle. God created mankind with emotions that enable us to feel and enjoy relationships. Healthy emotions like crying or laughing, seem to detoxify or drain anger and grief.

God's Candle

The reformation was kindled by a fire of passion. Hugh Latimer, the Bishop of Worcester (pronounced WOOS-ter) and a powerful reformation preacher, was born in 1487. His sermons encouraged people to pray and live holy lives. He resigned his position as bishop when the king would not allow the religious reforms that Latimer requested. His work was an integral part of what historians have called the Protestant Reformation.

Queen Mary arrested Hugh Latimer for heresy. He was tried, found guilty, and sentenced to be burned to death with his friend, Nicholas Ridley. On October 16, 1555, they were burned while tied to a stake. The flames that consumed their bodies could not extinguish their passionate faith. Latimer's last words were to encourage his friend: "Be of good cheer, Master Ridley, and play the man, for we shall this day light such a candle in England as I trust by God's grace

---

[65] Revelation 12:11

Passion - Fire

shall never be put out." [66]   And that is exactly what God did with these candles, His candles. He lit the light of reformation that birthed the Protestant religion.

Where is that passion today? Where is the churches' passion for the lost? Where is the passion to please God? Where is the passion that propels us to live Holy lives? Where? Are we so holy that we can live without Holy Spirit fire? Or has our carnal nature deceived us to the point that we are content without it? Where's the passion that drives us to pray, desperately longing for His presence in our lives? Where's the passion that compels us to forgive and give?

"A man without passion is only a latent force, only a possibility, like a stone waiting for the blow from the iron to give forth sparks." (Henri Frederic Amiel)

Carrying the Fire

In 1996, the Olympic summer games were held in the United States. The Olympic torch traveled across America to communities containing 90% of the America population. Ten thousand Americans were given the high honor of carrying the Olympic torch before it reached its final destination in Atlanta, Georgia. People of diverse ethnic groups and ages carrying the Olympic flame ran, walked, or rode their route to the next torch bearer and handed it off.[67] They traveled in all sorts of weather.

It was rainy when the flame came to my city. The wind was howling, and the rain pelted the runner as he crossed a tall bridge carrying the Olympic flame. Because the torch was carefully designed, the flame continued to burn in spite of the inclement weather. I waited to get a closer look at the runner with his famous torch. He was dripping wet and sloshing through puddles, but you should have seen his face; it was beaming. The dismal rain didn't

---

[66] http://justus.anglican.org/resources/bio/269.html (accessed June1, 2011)
[67] http://clinton6.nara.gov/1996/06/1996-06-21-remarks-at-departure-of-olympic-torch.html

douse his spirits. He held the torch triumphantly high. The crowds clapped and cheered; the torch was passing!

What an awesome experience. I was caught up in the ecstasy of the moment. We weren't there to see a person; we were there to see the Olympic Flame. Seeing the flame didn't change my life. As a matter of fact, I've never read any account that the Olympic flame made any significant difference in anyone's life.

But you have a higher calling than that of an Olympic flame bearer. You are called to carry the flame of Holy Spirit that will change people's lives. He brings hope to the hopeless. He offers light to the lost and healing to the sick. We are called to do the works of Christ through the power of Holy Spirit.

> Reader Harris states:
> The people who are living in the dispensation of the Spirit are fulfilling prophecy-and to forge the link of faith that joins prophecy and its fulfillment is a wonderful thing to do. Every man and woman filled with Holy Spirit, in this day, is doing that work, and is proving to angels, and demons, and men, and women aye, and children too—the truth of this Book, the reality of our God, the blessedness of being , as predicted, through a promised Saviour. These people live in the acts—not of the apostles, but of Holy Spirit; and they have found a kingdom that is "righteousness and peace and joy in the Holy Ghost. [68]

Carrying the Olympic Torch was a moving event; it was a public presentation that inspired national patriotism. But now it is a mere memory. Pentecost announced the arrival of the person of Holy Spirit. The events of the day are memorable, but the difference lies in the fact that everyday believers can experience their personal Pentecost, not a presentation for viewers but an empowering union that requires partnership and participation.

---

[68] Harris, *When He is Come*, 13.

Passion - Fire

I didn't get a good picture of the torch. Hoping to get a better picture, my daughter and I decided to go downtown, where the culminating Olympic Torch ceremony was taking place. We waited under the cover of a bridge along the river, where the runner was going to board a boat to go to the next destination on the route.

After waiting a while, I decided to make my way through the crowd to purchase a souvenir of the event when, suddenly, the orchestra began to play the National Anthem. The announcer's voice trembled with excitement: "It's coming! It's coming!" I stopped to place my hand over my heart. Tears coursed down my cheeks. It was an emotional moment, beyond national patriotism. My mind raced to the reality that one day Jesus will come; He is coming. Jesus is coming; I played the words in my mind as I prayed over the people silently. Jesus gave His life to redeem us. He's coming back again for a pure, radiant bride. The bride must be ready. The preparation that must take place for the bride to be ready is the work of Holy Spirit. Jesus proclaimed with the same passion as the announcer that day at the Olympic Torch Ceremony…Holy Spirit is coming. And He did come: to live in you and to cleanse and make you ready for life and the return of Christ.

Our Trademark

Usually, children point it out first. They see it long before they reach it. My kids always said, "Want French fry, Mommy!" Even the youngest child can identify it, long before they can read a single word. They recognize the McDonald's trademark golden arches, and squeal with delight if you stop or whine if you don't. The same is true for countless brands, from a Coach™ purse to a Nike™ shoe.

Christians have a trademark, too. It isn't a sign around our neck or a bumper sticker on our car. It's not a label or a logo tattooed to your body, but it is a mark that clearly identifies us as part of God's family. That identifying trademark is love. "Your love for one another will prove to the world that you are my disciples." (John 13:35)

Pentecost Lost

If love is our trademark, it must be the dye that colors everything we do. 1 Corinthians 13:1-3 very explicitly warns us that all giving, ministering, or serving is meaningless unless it flows out of love. Even extravagant gifts, like giving away all your money or giving up your life (like Hugh Latimer), must be an act of love, or it is a futile activity. That is a sobering reality. 1 Corinthians continues with a vivid description of love. Love is patient, polite, and kind. Love rejoices in truth; endures all things. Love believes and hopes.

The word "sunecho" in 2 Corinthians 5:14 is translated "compels" in NIV and "constrain" in KJV (NIV "For Christ's love compels us..." KJV "For the love of Christ constraineth us..."). The original word actually means both, although they seem to be antonyms. Compel means to drive while constrain means to hold back. Both are true in the same sense that a traffic light makes you stop and go. Sometimes love compels us to do things. And sometimes it prevents us.

1 Corinthians 13 describes the stops found in love. The stops of love illustrate what love is not. Love is not jealous, boastful, or proud. Love is not self-seeking. Love is not easily irritated. Love doesn't harbor a list of faults or wrongs. Love doesn't think the worst, doesn't rejoice when bad things happen. 1 Corinthians 13 is the measuring tape for gauging love. It is an accurate picture of what should be reflected in our lives.

Love is a powerful force. "We know how much God loves us, and we have put our trust in him. God is love, and all who live in love live in God, and God lives in them." (1 John 4:16) It doesn't say, "He has love," it says, "He is love." It is only the God kind of love that makes us recognizable as His child.

John 3:16 is such an important verse in the Bible, but it has become so familiar, we forget its significance. I want to remind you of its message. Because God loved, He gave. Not because we deserved it or earned it, but because He loved. You were the object of that love. He loves you more than you can imagine. I know you know that with your head, but mental assent is of little value.

I pray that from his glorious, unlimited resources he will give you mighty inner strength through his Holy Spirit. [17]And I pray that Christ will be more and more at home in your hearts as you trust in him. May your roots go down deep into the soil of God's marvelous love.[18]And may you have the power to understand, as all God's people should, how wide, how long, how high, and how deep his love really is. [19]May you experience the love of Christ, though it is so great you will never fully understand it. Then you will be filled with the fullness of life and power that comes from God.

---Ephesians 3:16-19

You can know and experience God's unfathomable love that reaches beyond human capacity in dimensions that are both diverse and increasing. Root yourself in His love, and let it nourish your attitudes and actions, like a white carnation is tinted red when placed in red water. Spend quiet time in His presence, allowing His peace and love to flow into your emotions. Love removes fear; so, clean and refresh your mind in the peaceful waters of His love. Allow God's love to kiss the broken places in your heart to bring healing and hope. Spectacular sunsets can be enjoyed almost anywhere, but you have to look at the sky. In similar fashion, you must look to His love. The elation of experiencing His love trickles and gushes out of relationship. His love can be enjoyed, but only to the extent that you receive it.

His love and the price He paid for you make you priceless. Knowing the value Almighty God places on you builds tremendous confidence. This confidence is one that our culture confuses with self-confidence, but a more accurate nomenclature would be God-confidence. Our culture has become so enamored with self-confidence that we have moved the "Big I" to idol status. The narcissistic flood that has ensued has destroyed lives and families.

> Dear friends, let us continue to love one another, for love comes from God. Anyone who loves is born of God and knows God. ⁸But anyone who does not love does not know God -- for God is love. ⁹God showed how much he loved us by sending his only Son into the world so that we might have eternal life through him. ¹⁰This is real love. It is not that we loved God, but that he loved us and sent his Son as a sacrifice to take away our sins. ¹¹Dear friends, since God loved us that much, we surely ought to love each other.
>
> ---1 John 4:7-11

We know we should love, but doing it is another matter. Our selfish, carnal nature wants to gratify our flesh. We love people who love us. We love people who make us feel good. But that isn't love. Even sinners love people who love them. God is requiring us to function out of a love that surpasses human capacity. The love described in 1 Corinthians 13 is wonderful when we think of receiving it but alarming when we realize we are expected to give that kind of love. I don't know about you, but I struggle with God's description of how my love should look. I get impatient. I have my lists of wrongs that have been done to me. While some people are easy to love, there are others who are a challenge for me. God's love doesn't have strings attached to conditions and neither should ours. The God kind of love is unconditional and comprehensive. It covers the faults of others instead of pointing them out.[69] God commands us to love people who don't deserve it and may not even want it! "Now you can have sincere love for each other as brothers and sisters because you were cleansed from your sins when you accepted the truth of the Good News. So see to it that you really do love each other intensely with all your hearts." (1Peter 1:22)

I can't do it. My love hardly resembles the real love described in1 Corinthians. It's impossible to love anyone like that. But the

---

[69] 1 Peter 4:8

impossible becomes possible as you partner with Holy Spirit. "And this expectation will not disappoint us. For we know how dearly God loves us because he has given us the Holy Spirit to fill our hearts with his love." (Romans 5:5) That is my desperate prayer, "God, pour in your love. I seriously crave this activity of your Spirit in my life." He pours His amazing love into our hearts, so we have love to enjoy and surplus to share with others. You can't give away something you don't have, so receive His love. When we are loved, we can love others. Receiving His love enlarges our capacity to love Him more. Everything we do must flow out of the reservoir of His love.

I remember going through a very difficult time. I was being treated unfairly. I was misunderstood and misrepresented. I struggled. I wanted to respond in like fashion, but I knew that was not God's best for me. I wanted to love these people, but I just didn't feel it! While I understand love is not a feeling, I struggled to line up my actions and especially my attitudes with God's plan: to love them. I prayed for what I perceived to be my enemies. I was desperate. I prayed, "Help me." Honestly, I didn't know how to pray, so I prayed in tongues.

One day as I was praying in tongues, God gave me a picture in my mind. I saw a picture of an oil refinery. There were tanks of all sizes, but immediately my attention was drawn to a towering tank in the center. The tall, fat tank had a large, hose-like pipe plugged into its side, which was attached to a smaller tank beside it. The oil from the giant tank flowed into the smaller tank.

I felt Holy Spirit speaking to my spirit, "Stay hooked up to me and I'll give you some of my love!" That was the answer I was looking for! I cannot be the source of love. I don't have that kind of love to give, but as God's love flows to me via the conduit of relationship with Him, I have His love to share.

One of the major ways to keep this Holy Spirit relationship connected and viable is through praying in tongues. Love is poured into our life through Holy Spirit. As we pray in tongues, we open the valve for love (plus everything else God has for us) to flow into our life or for people on our prayer list. His power to love has been given to us according to Romans 5:5.

New Glasses

Loving people sounds good, but what about un-loveable people? You do know they exist, don't you? There are some people who seem to enjoy making our lives miserable. How do we love people like that?

I have two suggestions for you. First, love is not a feeling. It is a choice. Second, change your focus. His love changes our attitudes and even how we view people.

Have you ever tried on sunglasses that were so dark you stumbled inside? Or have you put on sunglasses with yellow lens that made everything take on a golden hue? Love is a lens that you can see people through. When you love someone, you see them differently. You see through their bumbling and stumbling and see the effort beneath. You see the best instead of the worst. Sometimes, people's faults are blinding and almost debilitating, like the sunset glaring through your windshield as you head directly into the sun. I've had to pray, "God, help me to see through the lens of your love. Help me to see what you see." Take off the carnal glasses of criticism and jealousy. Pay attention. Guard your heart by guarding how you look at things. Are you looking through the lens of love or the dark lens of criticism?

As a mother, I appreciate the value people place on my children. It brings tremendous joy to me when someone does kind things for either of them. God shares that same kind of parental joy when people do good things for His children. I love God, and because He loves them, I choose to love them, too. As an act of my will, I choose to love. And, I choose to focus on their good traits instead of the bad ones.

Attracted to the Light

I must warn you that love has been counterfeited. Satan has twisted love and handed it back to humanity in a form so different from God's intent that it is unrecognizable. Love is paraded and depicted as perverted sex. Our culture has fallen for his lies. Our human need to be loved has enslaved people of all ages and races as they bow to its tyrannical demands. Twisted love, like a fire, can destroy or, like a magnet, can draw out the worst in a person

It wasn't quite daylight when I decided to turn off the front porch light. I had my hand on the light switch when I noticed movement outside. I stood still. Then I saw it again. It was a little bird snatching moths in his bill. I watched as he landed on the porch rail to gobble his wiggling breakfast. When I looked closer, I saw dozens of moths, moths of all sizes, flitting around the porch light. Moths are attracted to the light; even artificial light will draw a moth.

Love draws people like a light. We lose our light, our influence to draw people to Christ, when we lose our love. We've stopped attracting the lost because we've lost our love for Christ and for unbelievers. The Bible says in the last days we would become lovers of ourselves.[70] This prophecy is an accurate picture of today's narcissistic culture, which, by the way, has influenced the church as well. Because we have pushed precious Holy Spirit out of the church, we have very little love and very little light. While some believers have the light, they seem to cover it with timidity and political correctness. In the absence of the glorious Light of the world, people are drawn to the artificial light of popular idols: money, sex, and power. The artificial light of sin dazzles and dazes people as they follow satan happily down the road to destruction, like the moths on my front porch.

Watching the lost parade to hell should break our heart, but it doesn't. We look the other way and cross the street, like the priest in the story of the Good Samaritan. But, God's passion burning in our hearts leads us back to the altar of intercession, weeping for the lost. His passion makes us fall in love with sinners. It propels us to witness, give to missions, and care for the needy. William Robinson Clark makes a statement that I find deeply incriminating:

---

[70] 2 Timothy 3:2

Pentecost Lost

> In this great conflict, evil is intensely active; while in many cases the Church of Christ is criminally inactive. I say "criminally," because any Christian who is not filled with the Holy Ghost when he knows that that is his privilege becomes responsible for all that he might be and do for God, if endued with power from on high. How much religious work is to be met with around us! but comparatively HOW LITTLE FRUIT![71]

It's time for believers to repent and allow the fire of Holy Spirit to ignite our love. We don't have miracles flowing through our lives because we don't love - not because they have passed away.

Keep the Fire Burning

John the Baptist explained to his adherents that someone was coming who would baptize them with Holy Spirit and fire. Where is the fire? Is the modern church so effective and so wise we don't need it? Is the modern believer so pure and holy that the need for fire is extinct? Or, is it because our culture of microwaves and instant rice isn't willing to pay the price to have a fire burning on the altar of our hearts? Are Christians so full of love and spiritual energy that we don't need the fire?

The popularity of social networking on the internet exposes the innate craving for relationship. Beneath the cries for freedom and power is the hollow vacuum that only Jesus can fill. In spite of this drastic need, too many believers don't have enough fire to send a smoke signal, much less to warm sinners with the love of Christ. Our culture needs Jesus. The church is God's agent of evangelism, but the major outreach of too many churches is the church sign advertising the next service. Believers have become so comfortable in their little world that we don't even see lost people anymore.

---

[71] Harris, *When He is Come*, 69.

Passion - Fire

Revelation 2:1-7 is written to the Ephesian church. He commends them for their works but condemns their lack of love. Verse four says you've left your first love. Verse five says repent, do what you did before. I echo the words of Holy Scripture: we must repent. When we are full of self-love, we become so puffed up with pride that there is no room for God's love. It's time to fall passionately in love with God. We are barren believers because we are passionless believers. When we love with God's love, it draws people to Christ. Love is a force that can be felt. It is a love that goes beyond being a nice person.

A fire needs the same thing to keep burning that it needs to start burning. Revelation 2:4 states you don't love me like you did at first. Do you love God passionately and fervently? Do you love Him more now than when you first believed? Receive His love. You can't receive His love and not love Him back. You can't love God without loving your brother. God's love is the heat that keeps the fire burning.

> If someone says, "I love God," but hates a Christian brother or sister, that person is a liar; for if we don't love people we can see, how can we love God, whom we have not seen? [21] And God himself has commanded that we must love not only him but our Christian brothers and sisters, too.
> ---1 John 4:20-21

But more than heat is required - just ask a Boy Scout. Besides needing matches, you also need fuel and oxygen. To keep your spiritual fire burning, you need the same things. Your fuel is the Word of God. Be a diligent student of the Bible. Study the Scriptures, and allow the light of Holy Spirit to give you understanding. Fuel the fire by obeying what He shows you. Establish a place and a time to read your Bible, not because God demands it but because you need it. Then allow the breath of God to blow on your life through prayer, which should include praying and worshipping in the spirit.

Aunt Mae was a typical granny with glasses and grey hair, but there was something special about her. Aunt Mae was the reason the young mother questioned the words of her pastor, "Speaking in tongues is of the devil." Shirley's mind immediately raced to her Aunt Mae. She was a "tongue talking" Pentecostal, and there was nothing about her that was of the devil. This contradiction propelled Shirley to search the Bible tenaciously! She prayed as she read. She asked God to show her the truth. "God, if you have more for me, I want it." During this time-frame, her brother-in-law received the Baptism of Holy Spirit, so she asked him questions. A friend of a friend heard about Shirley's quest for more and agreed to meet with her. This lady began to unfold truths with Shirley that Holy Spirit was already showing her. Then the lady explained, "You can receive Holy Spirit, right here, right now, but you have to open your mouth." And, Shirley did. She received her personal Pentecost right there in the house where they were sitting, like Paul at Cornelius' house in Acts 10.

Like the book of Acts, she began to speak with tongues when she received Holy Spirit. But, she didn't stop; she prayed in tongues the whole way home. When her girls got home from school, she was anxious to share her great news. "I have something I want to tell you." With both young girls snuggled close, she unfolded the events of the day and how she had been filled with precious Holy Spirit. The youngest, Jennifer, went to her room even before her mom was completely through explaining what had happened to her. When she returned, her beaming face was streaked with tears, "I received Holy Spirit, too, Mom!"

Tongue

I am not a detailed person, so I see the bigger picture. I want to make it happen, like right now! But, I have decorated my home frequently enough to understand details are critical to turn a space into a room people will enjoy. The texture and quality of a fabric, the hue and tone of a color in a pillow, or the style and length of a drape only begin to illustrate the volume of details that make a room comfortable.

But, God is detailed. With each stroke of His pen, with each and every dash and dot, He deliberately arranges a symphony of events that help us discover principles for life that is pleasing to Him. The scene is shown in HD, "His Definition" or characterization, complete with surround sound of a mighty wind and supernatural events. They saw tongues of fire and spoke with tongues. There seems to be an emphasis on the influence that Holy Spirit wants to make on our speech.

While the tongue is a vital speech organ, your tongue isn't the origin of words, it only forms them. Words are mirrors to our soul reflecting our moral character, or hollow and meaningless talk when not followed with corresponding actions. When you are a kind person, your words will be kind. The words of an angry person are course and cruel.

Our words are powerful. Words can build up or tear down. One simple word can catapult us into action; or, if we scrawl an apostrophe and one little letter behind that same word, it can birth defeat before we ever start. The two words that alter attitude and destiny are can and can't. They are game changing words when they are believed. Let's look at Proverbs 18:21 (KJV): "Death and life are in the power of the tongue: and they that love it shall eat the fruit thereof."

It is unimaginable that a large, muscular horse can actually be turned and guided by a small bit in its mouth; or, that a small thin rudder can turn a boat to the left and right at will. As described in James 3, the tongue is such a small organ, yet it is so powerful. Your words not only mirror where you are mentally, emotionally, and spiritually, but they steer and influence your choices and your life.

Allow heaven to steer your course by praying in tongues instead of allowing fear-filled words to steer you. Every time you pray in tongues, you are yielding to Holy Spirit, like a horse yields to the bit in his mouth. Words emblaze emotions, encourage faith, or demolish dreams. Your words are influenced by your heart; and, your heart is affected by your words. When you change your words, you begin to effect change in your heart. God knows and understands a principle that we seem to trivialize: our words are important. We eat the harvest of the powerful seeds of our words.[72] While we can and should control and guard our words carefully, God has a larger strategy for words. He wants to help us speak words that will edify instead of destroy. He wants to give us a tool that bypasses human understanding of the power of Words and allows us to pray things and say things that we would never have the audacity or the idea to pray. Praying in the Spirit does that. You speak words that build you up - that builds others up.

> William Robinson Clark wrote:
> This brings us to consider briefly some of the blessings flowing from the Constitution of the Church, especially as indicated by the visible phenomena of Pentecost. The most remarkable of these was the appearance of "tongues parting asunder, like as of fire," resting upon each one of those present. A more significant symbol could hardly be imagined. Speech is, in truth, the highest gift of God to man; it is the expression of that reason which elevates him above the beasts that perish. The mere animal does not speak, because he does not possess that power of thought which utters itself in articulate language. So closely is the Word connected with the Reason that the same word stands for both in Greek, and it has even been debated whether the Logos in S. John should be translated The Reason or The Word.[73]

Even the Hem

When God instituted worship in the wilderness, every item, every color, and every thread was deliberately used to speak to the church age. He hid metaphors all the way down to the hem of the priest's garment. Moses was instructed by God that the fine linen robe was to be embellished with a golden bell and a pomegranate alternating

---

[72] Proverbs 18:21
[73] William Robinson Clark, *The Comforter,* Society for Promoting Christian Knowledge, 1875, 76.

around the entire hem.[74] "Aaron must wear it when he ministers. The sound of the bells will be heard when he enters the Holy Place before the LORD and when he comes out, so that he will not die." (Exodus 28:35) I believe, as do some theologians, that the golden bells are the vocal gifts that have been given to the church age. These vocal gifts that derive their origin from God, which are pure and holy and represented by the gold, include: speaking in tongues, interpretation of tongues, prophesy, word of knowledge, and word of wisdom as detailed in 1 Corinthians 12:7-11. But, the hem is embellished with more than bells. The picture is not complete without the fruit, the pomegranate. If the bell hits another bell, it clangs instead of ringing its sweet sound, which is the reason each bell needed to be separated from the next. The vocal gifts need to be accompanied with the fruit of love. I encourage you to heed Paul's admonition found in 1 Corinthians 14:1: "Follow after charity, and desire spiritual gifts, but rather that ye may prophesy." We need both the gifts of the Spirit and the fruit of the Spirit in operation in our lives. The gifts are gifts given to us by God; the fruit is grown and developed.

---

[74] Exodus 28:34; Exodus 39:26

Pentecost Lost

Think about it:

DUI: Dwell Under the Influence

Dear God, What do you want me to take away from this chapter?

Do I love God more than anything else?

Did I deliberately choose to walk out that love by loving people today?

Chapter Six

Purpose-Oil

Black Gold

It is hard to imagine life without cars and trucks or the crude oil that makes their mobility possible. In American history, the Seneca Indians made the first mention of black oil. It polluted their watering holes. They used blankets and pieces of cloth to soak up the nasty-tasting, oily scum off the top of their water sources, so they could drink the water. Creative, ingenious people tried to find uses for the sticky tar that oozed from the ground and clung to their feet and shoes. They concocted medicine from the seepage to treat kidney trouble, indigestion, and even ringworms. In the 1700's, the oily tar became known as rock oil. Later, it was called petroleum from the words "petra," which means rock, and "oleum," meaning oil. [75]

In the late 1850's, James Townsend heard a report that rock oil could be refined for use as lantern fuel and to lubricate wagon wheels. It was difficult to imagine that the thick, nasty stuff that seeped from the ground could be valuable. Rock oil production had commercial value only if they could acquire sufficient supplies of crude oil. Acquiring oil sounded like a great business opportunity, so Seneca Oil Company was formed, naming investor James Townsend as its president and Edwin Drake, a retired railroad man, to head up acquisition.

Everyone had seen the black seepage, but mining or removing this resource had never been done. Drake's research convinced him the oil deposits were there but offered no suggestion on how to remove it.

---

[75] http://www.pbs.org/wgbh/theymadeamerica/whomade/drake_hi.html

Pentecost Lost

After several different methods failed, he played with the idea of drilling by using the same process used in salt mining. Nobody thought it would work. Drilling for oil had never been done, but Drake had to at least try.

Drake purchased a steam engine and other equipment needed for drilling. As he continued to search for a driller, he built an engine house. Folks in Titusville, Pennsylvania, gossiped on street corners, calling him Crazy Drake. They liked Drake, but they mistook his passion for craziness.

Finally, William Smith, better known as Uncle Billy, a hardworking blacksmith, agreed to drill. Together, they built a wooden derrick or oilrig. They started drilling in late May. They worked six days a week because Drake refused to work on God's day. Repeatedly, the borehole filled with dirt, requiring them to re-drill the hole. Finally, they drove an iron pipe into the drill hole, inserted the drill bit into the pipe, and continued to drill. Their imaginative idea worked. The men persisted. They continued to drill deeper, day after day. They made mistakes but learned from them and drilled some more. Their acquired knowledge and persistence finally paid off when they struck oil on August 28, nearly seventy-feet down. Drake had discovered an innovative way to tap into the oil resources hidden in the ground. Soon, people were rushing from everywhere to make their fortune in Pennsylvania.[76]

Let's look at that story for a minute. Was oil a new discovery in the early 1800's? No. The folks in that town had seen the seepage all their lives, but they never understood its benefits, so they never pursued it until they recognized its value.

As a believer, I want to ask you two questions: Is the oil of Holy Spirit new? Has Holy Spirit only recently been discovered? The answer is the same to both of these questions: "No." We've seen Him seep into our churches or perhaps our lives every now and then. Although the Pentecostal outpouring took place over two thousand years ago, the expanded benefits come only when we recognize the

---

[76] http://www.pbs.org/wgbh/theymadeamerica/whomade/drake_hi.html

Purpose - Oil

purpose behind Pentecost, which propels us to pursue the person of Holy Spirit. These benefits and resources have been available to every believer in each generation since Pentecost. But, if the intrinsic value of Pentecost remains unknown and undesired, it will remain un-pursued.

Prior to the 1850's, people hated the thick, black stuff oozing out of the ground and ruining their shoes and clothing. They hated the taste of the oily scum that polluted their water. They had no idea how valuable crude oil would become. They could never have imagined that a civilization could become so totally dependent on oil, and that, without it, modern life would come to a screeching halt.

Similarly, the modern church fails to recognize the value of the Person of Pentecost. Expecting His presence seems eccentric. We feel inconvenienced when the pace of a service is slowed to include prayer for the sick. We don't want to be bothered by someone's need and seem repulsed when referring to a person who speaks in tongues. Unlike the chemist from Yale who unlocked the importance of rock oil, we refuse to discover the value of the infilling of Holy Spirit.

Do you see yourself in the group photograph of a redeemed yet immobilized crowd? Stir yourself. Go to the Scriptures for yourself. Prayerfully seek all God has for you. Refuse to stumble over the diamond because it is hidden in a rock. Like a chemist breaks down the components of a mixture, break down the Scriptures. Discover who Holy Spirit is. Discover the benefits He brings to your life and your ministry. Discover how to tap into the richness of relationship that comes from knowing Him personally. It seems God wants you to unwrap who He is, like a valuable present is unwrapped. When you un-wrap the outer box, you get a clue as to who He is; but, there's also another wrapped box inside. This process of un-wrapping and seeking Him continues on and on and on. It is a continual process of discovery. God wants you to know Him. God wants to reveal Himself to you, and that's why He sent Holy Spirit.

Every area of our lives is affected by oil and the fuel products produced from it. Trucks and trains, transporting groceries and clothing to the local stores where you shop, are fueled by oil products.

Pentecost Lost

The yellow caterpillar that carries hundreds of children to school is fueled by an oil product. Factories producing a variety of products use oil in the manufacturing process. Oil is used inside engines to reduce friction, causing the parts to last longer and operate more efficiently. Farms tractors and combines used in food production are fueled by oil products. The machinery that cuts the trees and turns the wood into furniture, houses, and paper goods are all fueled by oil products. In varying degrees and functions, everything we have and do is affected by oil products. Modern civilization needs oil for almost everything. Without oil, life as we know it would cease! While the people of the 1840's didn't see its value, we understand its purpose, and we value the benefits of oil.

Yes, we need oil. Yet far more desperately than we can fathom, even beyond our apparent need of petroleum, we need the oil of Holy Spirit. In the Bible, oil is a picture of Holy Spirit. Just like a car needs gasoline, believers need the fuel of Holy Spirit's ability and energy in their lives. Like a lamp needs oil, like a salad dressing needs oil, like an engine needs oil, we need the oil of Holy Spirit.

The people of the Bible didn't use the black crude oil variety that modern civilization requires. They used olive oil in almost every facet of their lives. They cooked with it, ate it in their food, put it in their lamps, and anointed their skin with it. The root word, "mashack," is used 151 times in the Bible. It means to anoint or smear with oil. Athletes of ancient Greece smeared oil on themselves before they ran a race. Fragrant, holy oil was a vital part of their worship as well. Anointing was more than someone's clever idea, even more than a symbolic gesture. Anointing was a directive from God. Oil is used to produce energy, transform oil into fuel, and nourish a nation. Holy Spirit does the same for the church.

Who Needs the Anointing?

According to the Bible, who needs Holy Spirit anointing? God's directive arrived with explicit details outlining guidelines for anointing the priests before they began their service to both God and the people. First, the priest's right ear, right thumb, and right toe were anointed with blood as a reminder that they must be cleansed by the blood of the sacrificial lamb. (Exodus 29:20) You can remember it this way. The priest's ear was anointed to hear, his thumb so he wouldn't be a bum, and his toe so he could go. God wanted to help the priest hear, serve, and go in a direction that was pleasing to Him. God knew the priest would need His help. Thus, the holy anointing oil was sprinkled on the priest and his clothes. (Exodus 29:21) The anointing was an activity of faith and obedience that reminded the priest he was dependent on Almighty God for success. The fragrant oil, mixed with very expensive spices, produced a delightful, sensual symphony that was used singularly as holy anointing oil.[77]

When my first granddaughter was a little baby, I had the privilege of helping care for her. After her bath, I would slather her with baby lotion, dress her in a soft sleeper, and wrap her in a fluffy blanket. Clean and sweet smelling, warm and drowsy, she cuddled in my arms. As I kissed those soft, sweet cheeks, the smell was wonderful. Those moments remain precious to me.

Your worship is like a sweet fragrance to God. When you draw near to God in sincere, heartfelt praise and worship, I wonder if it makes Him feel like I felt holding that precious, sweet-smelling baby in my arms. I know He loves your worship. He is so wonderful and so absolutely worthy of your worship. He is both powerful and wise. As you worship Him, sometimes you will find that your native language is just too limiting. You will run out of words to express how much you love Him. You will find words are totally inadequate. Sometimes, it is as if Holy Spirit leans in and says something like, "I'll lend you some of my words!" Then, you change from worshipping God in your language to worshipping God in the spirit. This higher dimension of worship should become part of your regular prayer time. Don't be in a hurry. Linger and soak in His presence. It may feel

---

[77]Exodus 30:25 "Make these into a sacred anointing oil, a fragrant blend, the work of a perfumer. It will be the sacred anointing oil."

awkward if you are dry spiritually; like a dry sponge, it may take a little soaking to soften, but after that, it can absorb the liquid.

The early Church experienced a surprising benefit from Holy Spirit infilling - joy. "Thou hast loved righteousness, and hated iniquity; therefore God, even thy God, hath anointed thee with the oil of gladness above thy fellows." (Hebrews 1:9) I love that picture: the oil of joy. His amazing joy is so deep that it finds its root in the depths of the love and care of Almighty God. His joy gives us strength and rejuvenates our vitality. At Pentecost, their joyful antics looked like "a whole lot of partying was going on." There was a party, but it was different than what the world experiences. They were accused of being drunk, and they were. They were drunk on new wine that produced incredible joy! I will be the first to agree that the presence of God makes you feel like you have a party going on inside of you. I love His presence because it brings incredible joy.

If you are not experiencing His energizing joy, then begin to declare Romans 15:13. Say, "Father, I thank you that the God of all hope fills me with all joy and peace in believing that I may abound with hope through the power of the Holy Ghost." Declare this promise of God until you see the fruit of it in your life. The last part of Nehemiah 8:10 reads, "...for the joy of the LORD is your strength." There is strength in joy. Don't be robbed of this benefit.

I love to feel the anointing; it brings me great joy. I wish I could describe the feeling I experience when the anointing rests on me as I speak or preach. I love the surge of anointing as I pray over someone, and they experience His presence and joy. Yet, the anointing comes with a purpose. Experience the joy, but pursue His purpose behind the anointing. Priests ministered to God through worship and to people by helping them connect with God. Holy Spirit anointing makes our ministry to people more effective.

Kings

Kings were anointed in the Bible. David, the second king of Israel and my favorite king, was anointed three times before assuming his

Purpose - Oil

reign over the nation of Israel. Samuel was the first to anoint him. (1 Samuel 16:13) God instructed Samuel to anoint a son of Jesse to be the next king while King Saul still reigned on the throne. Samuel went to Jesse's house expecting to find a man with a kingly grace and persona. You can imagine Jesse's anxiety and then his excitement when he understood his special visitor came as a guest. It was a huge honor to have the nation's most powerful religious leader visit his home – like having a visit from the President of the United States or the Queen of England. One by one, Jesse introduced his sons to Samuel. And one by one, God said, "This is not the one." When the line-up of sons had passed, Samuel was baffled. "Is this all of your sons?"

"No, sir," Jesse answered. "The youngest is away caring for the sheep."

"Send for him immediately. We won't eat until he arrives," Samuel instructed.

Can you imagine being excluded from this event by your parents? Everyone saw an insignificant kid, a mere shepherd boy, as someone totally inept, but God saw more - a king. God told Samuel to anoint David to be King. David was not the people's choice, but he was God's choice. Samuel emptied the animal horn containing fragrant anointing oil over the bewildered young man's head. David was anointed with a promise to *prepare* him for his future. Don't allow people's opinion of you to limit your faith or your reach. God has treasures hidden in you that only faith and obedience will release. [78]

Secondly, he was anointed by his heritage, the tribe of Judah. Judah means praise. David lived up to his family name. He was a mighty man of *praise* and worship, both privately and publicly.[79]

Lastly, David was anointed and accepted as king by the nation.[80] He was anointed to lead and *preserve* the nation of Israel. Jesus said that we are the salt - the preservative - leading people away from the

---

[78] Story of Samuel anointing David is found in 1 Samuel 16:1-13
[79] 2 Samuel 2:4
[80] 2 Samuel 5:3

decaying effects of sin. Each anointing prepared him for a different level of ministry: Prepare; Praise; Preserve.

Prepare yourself by meditating on Scripture. Offer your praise purposely and sincerely. Be a preservative in a culture of critics, a preservative that prevents the destruction of the souls of man by pointing them to Christ.

Christ the Anointed One

Not only were both kings and priests anointed, Jesus was anointed. All four gospels record Jesus' supernatural anointing in the Jordan River. (Matthew 3:16; Mark 1:10; Luke 3:22; John 1:32) Even His name, Christ, means "Anointed One." Scripture clearly tells us that Jesus was anointed by God.

> You know what happened all through Judea, beginning in Galilee after John the Baptist began preaching. [38]And no doubt you know that God anointed Jesus of Nazareth with the Holy Spirit and with power. Then Jesus went around doing good and healing all who were oppressed by the devil, for God was with him.
>
> ---Acts 10:37-38

These verses describe what the anointing looked like as it flowed through the life of Jesus: "...he went around doing good and healing all..." This Holy Spirit anointing that came on Jesus was not just an activity but an impartation of power to do the works of the Father. The anointing came for a purpose.

> When he came to the village of Nazareth, his boyhood home, he went as usual to the synagogue on the Sabbath and stood up to read the Scriptures. [17]The scroll containing the messages of Isaiah the prophet was handed to him, and he unrolled the scroll to the place where it says: [18]'The Spirit of the Lord is upon me, for he has appointed me to preach Good News to the poor. He has sent me to proclaim that captives

Purpose - Oil

will be released, that the blind will see, that the downtrodden will be freed from their oppressors, [19]and that the time of the Lord's favor has come.' [20]He rolled up the scroll, handed it back to the attendant, and sat down. Everyone in the synagogue stared at him intently. [21]Then he said, "This Scripture has come true today before your very eyes!

---Luke 4:16-21

In this Scripture, Jesus explained the purpose behind the anointing that rested on His life. (Luke 4:16-21) He purposefully located the verse we read in Isaiah 61:1 and began to read aloud, "The Lord has anointed me to…"

Bring good news
Comfort broken hearted
Proclaim liberty to captives
Proclaim prisoner's release
Declare God's favor
Announce a Divine exchange

When he finished reading, He sat down. Every eye turned to look at Him, so Jesus explained, "Today that Scripture is fulfilled in me." Jesus explained that His life and ministry were made possible by the anointing of Holy Spirit. This anointing enabled Him to fulfill Isaiah 61:1-3. Jesus was anointed by the Father with Holy Spirit to do the things He saw His Father do. The ultimate work or purpose behind the anointing was for people to believe. "Jesus told them, 'This is what God wants you to do: Believe in the one he has sent.'" (John 6:29) Jesus, through the power of Holy Spirit, confirmed the Word of God through signs and wonders. The purpose exceeded satisfying the people's temporal needs to becoming a signpost leading them to believe on Jesus.

If Jesus needed signs and wonders to guide people to the truth, don't we need them in our modern culture? God understood a light was needed to guide unbelievers to God, so He sent precious Holy Spirit to fuel believers to be a convincing testimony of the power of God through amazing miracles. The same Holy Spirit that anointed Jesus is available to you. "The truth is, anyone who believes in me will do the same works I have done, and even greater works, because I am going to be with the Father." (John 14:12)

Greater works than Jesus! Think about that for a minute. What kind of works did Jesus do? He healed the lame, opened blind eyes, and raised the dead. Yet, He promised that we would do greater works. How could this be possible? Because the same Holy Spirit that filled Jesus can fill believers everywhere, so the works of Jesus could be multiplied again and again all over the world.

Andrew Murray said:
> I will meditate and be still, until something of the overwhelming glory of the truth fall upon me, and faith begin to realize it: I am His Temple, and in the secret place He sits upon the throne. I do now tremblingly accept the blessed truth: God the Spirit; Holy Spirit; who is God Almighty dwells in me O my Father, reveal within me what it means, lest I sin against Thee by saying it and not living it.[81]

We can be enabled to do the works of Christ by Holy Spirit. Pentecost was the message on the screen of time that announced the enabling power of precious Holy Spirit. He gave us Holy Spirit because we need the anointing to do the works of Christ in this generation.

"In the same way, let your good deeds shine out for all to see, so that everyone will praise your heavenly Father." (Matthew 5:16) It is important that we understand God designed us to live as a lamp, not a candle. Too many people "burn out" because they live and serve out of their personal abilities and talents. If, instead, you live dependent on the Spirit of God flowing into you, like oil in a lamp, your light will shine as long as you have oil. Your goodness is not sufficient to solve man's greatest need, but when your light points people to Jesus, they find their solution.

The Sistine Chapel is noted world-wide for its magnificent Michelangelo-frescoed ceiling. Years of deterioration had faded its

---

[81]Chadwick, *The Way to Pentecost*, 17

beauty, and it had to be repaired. Everything in this world is going to fade away, but God is calling you to build something that will never fade or deteriorate. He is calling you to touch people with the love and power of God. This can only be done as you connect to God and allow precious Holy Spirit to flow through you to other people. His glory will rest on you in a way that is recognizable.

The Anointing Today

So far, we have seen that priests, kings, and Jesus needed the anointing. It is arguably true that ministers and political leaders need God's presence and help, which we have described as the Holy Spirit anointing. But what about ordinary people; can they experience the anointing, also?

I was attending a funeral the first time I recognized the anointing on a person. After several ministers had spoken briefly, an older, wrinkled man moved slowly behind the microphone to pray. I bowed my head in respect. The fragile-looking, southern gentleman began to pray. As I listened, the man's voice changed. There was a strength or authority that came into the man's voice. He sounded so different I thought maybe someone different had stepped to the microphone, so I peeked to see who was praying. The older gentleman was still there, but the anointing had affected his voice. He even stood straighter and taller. There was a power in his prayer that I had never sensed from anyone before.

That elderly gentleman whetted my appetite for the anointing. I've experienced it in so many areas of my life. I've tapped into that anointing to handle discipline issues with my children. I've experienced the anointing as a gentle impression guiding me where to look for something or to drive a different route home. Also, I've experienced the anointing, as a prompting, to make a phone call or to carry the neighbor next door a cake. I've felt it surge through me as I prayed for people at a church altar or on the telephone. I've heard it resonate in my voice as I spoke the Word of God to children and adults. I've heard myself praying about things that I wouldn't normally pray about, and in such specific ways that I was surprised. I realized it was Holy Spirit giving me insight how to pray. The anointing comes in practical and spiritual ways to produce both practical and spiritual solutions.

Christian means "like Christ." If we are going to be like Christ, then we must be anointed or smeared with the oil of Holy Spirit. "It is God who gives us, along with you, the ability to stand firm for Christ. He has commissioned us..." (2 Corinthians 1:21) He is talking about us in this verse. The anointing is not reserved and limited to priests or preachers. It is not conserved for kings and presidents. We need the anointing to teach school, operate machinery, run a business, and parent our children. Don't misunderstand me; we can do all these things without the anointing; but, we can do it better with the anointing. Holy Spirit wants to infiltrate every area of our life.

Is It Only For Special People?

Let me show you from Matthew 22:2-14 that the anointing is not reserved for only special people. I have enjoyed and shared with friends and family the beautiful weddings of my children. I can understand the king's excitement as he extended an invitation to the upcoming wedding feast. His circle of friends rudely refused the invitation with brazen disrespect. The king's servants were beaten and murdered. Livid, the king sent retribution. Again, his servants were sent to invite guests. However, this time the invitation was broadcast from street corners and intersections to anyone who wanted to attend the wedding. The banquet room was filled with guests, all clothed in beautiful wedding garments provided by the king. One guest, without the king's wedding garment, was immediately removed. This takes us to the infamous verse, "Many are called, but few are chosen." (Matthew 22:14) In the context of this story, who are the chosen ones? They are the ones who went to the wedding wearing the king's wedding attire. They weren't chosen because they were smart, rich, or beautiful. They were chosen because they responded to the king's invitation.

Purpose - Oil

The thinking of our modern culture has seeped into the church. We think God's selection criteria are talent and wealth; neither one is on His priority list. We are chosen because God loves us. The New Covenant qualifier is to accept Jesus as Savior and put on His robe of righteousness, which is freely given to us. We are chosen because we respond to His invitation and not because of who we are. God's not looking for ability - He's looking for avail-ability.

> Remember, dear brothers and sisters, that few of you were wise in the world's eyes, or powerful, or wealthy when God called you. [27]Instead, God deliberately chose things the world considers foolish in order to shame those who think they are wise. And he chose those who are powerless to shame those who are powerful. [28]God chose things despised by the world, things counted as nothing at all, and used them to bring to nothing what the world considers important, [29]so that no one can ever boast in the presence of God.
> ---1 Corinthians 1:26-29

Only a Tomato Can

They married during the depression. While every gift was precious to the poor couple, one gift stood out as the young bride's absolute favorite treasure--a beautiful set of fine crystal goblets. She could hardly imagine owning anything so beautiful. After a while, they moved into a small frame house. There she carefully placed the fragile goblets on the top shelf in the kitchen cabinet.

It wasn't long until the couple started their family. One after another, six little bundles of joy were added to the family. Instead of buying glasses, most folks washed the last little globs of jelly out of the jelly jar and used it for a drinking glass. As each child grew tall enough to climb onto the counter top and get their own glass out of the cabinet, they would be instructed: "You can use any jelly glass you want, but never, ever, touch the goblets on the top shelf. They're real crystal, you know!" The beautiful, fine crystal goblets remained safe on the top shelf.

Pentecost Lost

It gets hot in Alabama in the summer time, and kids get awfully thirsty. When the kids in this poor family got thirsty, they raced to the old water pump in the back yard.

Plopped upside down on top of the pump was a tomato can. Hand-operated can openers were hard to use. They cranked and chewed around the can slowly, cramping your hand as you cut the can open. Because opening the can was so much work, the lid was usually left attached to the can on one side. So, their daddy had taken a pair of pliers and carefully curled the sharp edges of the lid over to make a smooth handle for their homemade cup.

There they pumped the handle up and down until the refreshing, cool water gurgled into the homemade cup. The tomato can was passed around, refilled, and passed again and again until everyone's thirst was quenched. The exquisite, crystal goblets remained on the shelf while an ordinary tomato can brought water to thirsty kids. The crystal goblets, both beautiful and expensive, were never used.

Maybe you feel like an ordinary tomato can. That's a good thing! I am convinced God is not looking for crystal goblets. He is looking for ordinary tomato cans He can fill with His glory. Don't forget, the tomato can was only useful when it was filled. You cannot complete your destiny empty, so be filled. Being filled is not a one-time experience, but a lifelong journey. Be filled with all the fullness of God. God has called and chosen you.

> "But you are not like that, for you are a chosen people. You are a kingdom of priests, God's holy nation, his very own possession. This is so you can show others the goodness of God, for he called you out of the darkness into his wonderful light."
>
> ---1 Peter 2:9

God's not looking at what you can't do. Instead, your potential is viewed through the lens of what you can do through the power of Holy Spirit flowing through you.

"You didn't choose me. I chose you. I appointed you to go and produce fruit that will last, so that the Father will give you whatever you ask for, using my name." (John 15:16)

Stay Connected

I have a warm, outgoing friend who tends to get distracted easily. One day, she pulled into a service station, swiped her credit card, and removed the nozzle to fill her tank with gas. She locked the trigger on the nozzle, so it would maintain a constant gas flow, leaving her free to meet and greet. She talked to everyone within earshot until she noticed the dollar and cents digits on the gas pump had stopped moving, which was her clue to end her chat. She waved goodbye and climbed into her car to leave.

One lady, standing at a nearby pump, waved frantically. A man at another pump honked his horn. My friend smiled warmly and returned the wave, thinking to herself, "What friendly folks!"

When she arrived home, her husband came out to unload the trunk while she unloaded the back seat. When she returned to grab a second load from the car, he was still standing in the same place - shaking his head. She saw the look on his face first. Then, she saw the nozzle; she had driven off with the nozzle still in her gas tank. I know what you are thinking, and I agree. She's more than a little ditzy!

My friend would be the first to tell you that it's not possible to stay hooked up to a constant supply of gas. Yet, it is possible to stay hooked up to a constant supply of the oil of Holy Spirit because He lives in you. Develop an awareness of the presence of God. Connect through prayer and praise. Turn on the supply valve through faith.

The precious things of God do not come to disengaged Christians. It's not enough to connect at church occasionally. The deep things of God do not come to uncommitted believers. They come to people who are passionate about the things of God. What do passionate people look like? They are people who believe God, obey Him, and humbly serve Him. Do you want to be an agent of change? You have been called by God to make a difference in your world. This can only take place as Holy Spirit enables you.

Two Olive Trees

We see this principle of uninterrupted connection illustrated as Zechariah and Zerubbabel tried to complete their difficult assignment. Zechariah had the daunting task of mobilizing the emancipated Jews to rebuild the altar and the temple of the Lord. The rubble and ruin that remained from the city's destruction was demoralizing. It seemed that the Jews were being distracted and hindered on every front, until finally all construction came to a total stop.[82] They had a vision to rebuild, but they could only sit with rubble all around them and wait. They must have felt powerless and terribly discouraged. In Zechariah 4, God gave Zechariah a vision of a golden candlestick flanked on both sides by an olive tree.

> [6]Then he said to me, "This is what the LORD says to Zerubbabel: It is not by force nor by strength, but by my Spirit, says the LORD Almighty. [7]Nothing, not even a mighty mountain, will stand in Zerubbabel's way; it will flatten out before him! Then Zerubbabel will set the final stone of the Temple in place, and the people will shout: 'May God bless it! May God bless it!'
> ---Zechariah 4:6-7

He wanted to assure Zerubbabel that he would do more than simply lay a foundation; he would complete construction. God wanted Zerubbabel to recognize the job required more strength or power than he could muster. Zerubbabel saw the task, but what he needed to see was his source - God's Spirit - Who would enable him to finish the task.

---

[82] Ezra 4:4, 21

Purpose - Oil

Zechariah asked the angel, "What are the two olive trees?" A major responsibility for a priest was to fuel the lamp in the holy place with pure, fresh oil, so it would burn continuously. But, the lamp Zechariah saw was not tended by a priest. The oil was funneled directly from two living olive trees into the golden lamp. Zechariah saw an illustration of miraculous supply to help him visualize God as his source.

The vision, while both inspiring and encouraging to Zerubbabel and Zechariah, was also a prophetic picture for the modern church. Let's look at the picture again. The prophetic picture represented by the golden candlestick is the Church. The lamp stand was gold because it is God's Church - not a building but a holy habitation for His Spirit. The church was symbolized as a candlestick because it should be a light in a dark world. John Wesley said:

> All which is an emblem of the church, made of pure gold; to be a light in the world; to shine as lamps that continually burn, maintained with pure oil, distilled from the olive - trees, not pressed out by man, but continually, abundantly, and freely flowing from God.[83]

But, why did the vision include two olive trees? What was God saying with this clue? Even the prophet, to whom the vision was given, asked for clarification. John Wesley's commentary for Zechariah 4:14 states: "The two anointed ones - Christ and Holy Spirit. The Son was to be sent by the Father, and so was the Holy Ghost."[84] This is really, really important. The Church needs two trees to burn brightly in the end time. We desperately need Jesus, the living Word, and the living Holy Spirit.

But, the mystery in this picture continues to unfold. When olive oil is produced, the olives are removed from the trees. Did you notice

---

[83]John Wesley's commentary on the whole Bible was produced between 1754 and 1765. http://www.biblestudytools.com/commentaries/wesleys-explanatory-notes/zechariah/zechariah-4.html (accessed June 1, 2011)
[84]Ibid.

that the oil in this picture did not come from lifeless fruit but a living tree? What is the significance of oil from an olive tree, instead of oil from an olive? The significance is life. Our faith is not rooted in a dead hero, but a living, risen Savior. Our relationship is not built on a distant memory, but a personal indwelling. He is alive with a viable voice speaking and a watchful eye guiding. As a tender shepherd, He is both nourishing and protecting. It is comparable to the difference between viewing a photograph of a garden and taking a stroll through that fragrant garden, listening to the birds and exploring exotic waterfalls, with the love of your life. Far too many believers have never experienced anything beyond the photograph they glimpse in Scripture.

I Want More

In a time of great spiritual dissatisfaction, I began to cry out to God for more of His anointing in my life. I had some powerful, godly saints lay hands on me and pray that the anointing would increase in my life. Yet, I failed to experience a major difference in the anointing. I talked with a powerful minister of international prominence, and he encouraged me to step out in faith. He said, "The more you pray for people, the more results you will see." I understood his suggestion, embraced it, and obeyed it, but there was still no major change.

Finally, a turning point in my life came when I realized the root of my lack was unbelief. Notice I said, my lack, not God's. It was easy for me to believe God could use someone else. But, I knew my faults and my weaknesses. I had a long list of personal limitations and inabilities. I recognized that the same fear that birthed disobedience in the Israelites and kept them out of the Promised Land, leading to their life of unfulfilled destiny, was keeping me out of my Promised Land - a powerful anointing on the activities I had been called to do. I always thought God understood and excused my fear. I fed my fear with religious excuses. "I want to be used of God, but I'm afraid. I don't want to do the wrong thing, so I won't do anything." I prayed, but I was moored to the fear: "What if nothing happens?"

I had to get honest with myself. Did God pet the Israelites' fear? Do you really think God responded something like, "Oh, my! You're afraid! That's so sad. You sit right here. You don't have to fight those mean ole giants, you poor baby!" Of course not! They were robbed by their fear.

I saw myself just like the Israelites, fearful and unbelieving. Instead of making excuses, I asked God to forgive me, and I changed what I was doing. Realizing that only God can perform miracles, I chose to activate my faith and plug into His resources through intercession, expecting God to answer. I began to feed my faith and starve my fears. I must believe if I want to please Him. "So, you see, it is impossible to please God without faith. Anyone who wants to come to him must believe that there is a God and that he rewards those who sincerely seek him." (Hebrews 11:6) When I decided to cut the rope on my fears, the anointing increased.

Do you believe God will anoint you? Go to the root of your fear and repent. Believe the promises of Scripture. God wants to anoint you. Step out in obedient faith.

Conduits Not Containers

God wants believers to be healthy, both spiritually and physically (3 John 1:2). La Cucina Italiana reports that extra-virgin olive oil is the most digestible of the edible fats. It helps your body to absorb vitamins A, D, and K. It slows down the aging process. Olive oil helps keep you healthy by supporting better digestion and both liver and intestinal functions.[85]

In James 5:14-15, we see an activity of faith using the anointing oil. I hope you will mark and memorize these verses. "Are any among you sick? They should call for the elders of the church and have them pray over them, anointing them with oil in the name of the Lord. [15] And their prayer offered in faith will heal the sick, and the Lord will make them well. And anyone who has committed sins will be forgiven."

---

[85] http://en.wikipedia.org/wiki/Olive_oil (accessed June 2, 2011)

Pentecost Lost

The instructions are very clear in scripture what to do when people are sick:
1. Call for the elders.
2. Anoint with oil.
3. Pray.

What will the prayer of faith do? Make them well.

I am not trying to infer there is magical power in oil. Yet, I am confident there is power in obedience, which includes the directives outlined in James. We can be like Naaman, who wanted his miracle to arrive via the hand of a mighty prophet of God with spectacular fanfare instead of the drudgery of dipping seven times in a ridiculously muddy Jordan River[86]. I love this phrase (which came from a source unknown to me): "We can doubt and do without; or we can believe and receive." When we believe, we deliberately line up our activities with the Bible to receive the miracles that are an overflow of the Spirit of God in our lives.

Did Edwin Drake create the oil? No. He only drilled down to the oil, inserting pipe for the oil to flow through. That is what God intended for His church to do. We must tap into the oil of Holy Spirit through prayer, so His Spirit can flow through us to touch a needy world.

Let me explain it with a personal example. I want to see people healed. I believe it is God's will to heal the sick, yet everyone I pray for does not get healed. Should I quit praying for the sick because someone did not get healed? No, I can't stop. My faith is not based on results or personal experience. I must base my life on the Word of God. If I want to have the results Jesus did, then I must do the things Jesus did. While I understand that the gifts of Holy Spirit are distributed by God as He chooses, I also believe that there are things that will increase their flow out of my life. Faith will bring increase. Love will bring increase because compassion unlocks the heart of God. While everything doesn't hinge on me and on my faith, I believe

---

[86] 2 Kings 5:11-14

there are things that will hinder the flow of Holy Spirit as well.[87] I search my heart to be sure there is nothing that is hindering the flow. I build my faith, and I continue to pray healing scriptures over needs.

We need to be very careful that we maintain a conduit mentality instead of a container mentality. A container mentality hoards for personal use, but a conduit is a container with both ends open. One end of the conduit is connected to the resources and life of God and the other end pours out to others. It is easy to forget that we are more than containers; we are conduits for Holy Spirit to flow through. "Jesus answered, 'The work of God is this: to believe in the one he has sent.'" (John 6:29 NIV) We must not lose focus of the purpose behind His presence in our life. His presence is definitely for our benefit, but it is also to cause unbelievers to believe on Christ.

Never lose sight of the reality that you are powerless to meet the deepest needs of people. Only as you stay connected to God's vast supply will you be a conduit for needs to be met. You can see God heal the sick. You can see brokenhearted people filled with hope and encouragement. You can see alcoholics set free. There are so many things that God wants to do through you to minister His grace in the lives of others.

After empting oil from a measuring cup into cake batter, is the cup the same as before you poured the oil into it? No, the cup will be oily even after the cup has been emptied. That is what happens to us. As we become a pipe for precious Holy Spirit to flow through, He makes us oily. The benefits that flow through us to bless others are resident to bless us as well.

Clogged?

It is up to us to keep the flow flowing! I experienced a season in my life when the anointing stopped flowing, as if it were clogged up by something. It was a tragic season; the manifest anointing lifted off my ministry. Let me share the details with you.

---

[87] Mark 6:5

Pentecost Lost

I was pregnant with my first baby. It was a very busy time for me, personally, and for the church. Our pastor was an elderly man, full of vim and vigor, but overwhelmed with the task of building a large, new church. The church had relocated, which was a battle in itself. He was encouraging members to help with the construction as much as possible to keep construction costs low. Often, he found himself with only a handful of men, struggling to get the building completed. He was also a micro-manager. Every decision had to come across his desk. I was a volunteer, yet I worked long hours to have a first-class children's ministry. We were reaching into the community with a large bus ministry. My team used a variety of effective teaching methods to keep the program exciting. As my delivery date approached, I needed someone to take my place. I had everything organized; all the materials were ready; all the teams were ready to go; but I didn't have my replacement in place. I suggested several names, but I couldn't get a decision from my pastor, so I couldn't ask them to serve. It was a very stressful situation.

Things only got worse when we moved into the new church. Everything was grand: the best carpet; dazzling, domed sky-light; huge and magnificent chandelier in the lobby. The wallpaper was stunning. Everything was decorated exquisitely - until you made your way to the back of the church to the children's department. There, the floors were bare. One of the deacons decided we couldn't leave the floor bare; so, he purchased and had indoor-outdoor carpet installed. There wasn't money for curriculum, which wasn't a new problem, but now the issue made me angry. I didn't say anything to anyone. But, I was upset with my pastor. I felt my ministry was suffering because his priorities were out of balance. When I went to church, I sat under the balcony and complained in my mind. I didn't worship. While I never stopped loving God, my relationship with Him suffered. I allowed the flow of God's Spirit to stop in my life. Without realizing it, I was clutching my offense. A wrong attitude toward my pastor festered in my heart, although I was sure no one knew what was happening.

Things in children's church were different. I preached, but there was no anointing. I studied and prayed. My object lessons were good, and my stories were interesting, but they fell flat. Our puppet skits were entertaining, but the laughter wasn't enough. I missed the anointing: the presence of Holy Spirit that brings conviction and comprehension. Now, people can say what they want to say, but I've ministered with the anointing and I've ministered without it, and I don't ever want to minister without it again. The anointing doesn't make you loud, but it does make you passionate, powerful, and convincing. I repented to God. Then, I went to my pastor and asked for his forgiveness. Everything was back in order, or so I thought, but several months passed before the anointing began to flow again.

This experience taught me two things very clearly. First, the anointing is extremely precious and valuable to me. I diligently guard the anointing. Second, the flow of anointing can be obstructed or hindered by disobedience, fear, and wrong attitudes.

Uncap the Well

There are many believers who have received precious Holy Spirit without experiencing His overflow or His grace flowing out. Their well seems to be capped. Imagine with me that oil is discovered on your property; nice thought, isn't it! The next step is to drill the well. The process is completed. The oil reservoir is significant. There is no doubt that your well has enormous production potential. But, instead of pumping the oil out of the ground, you cap the well. Ignoring its potential to enrich your life, you are content to let it remain untapped and its benefits unused. Crazy! It doesn't make sense to me.

But would it be too farfetched to think that that is exactly what happens far too frequently in churches? I mean, haven't you seen people who go to a revival, receive the infilling of Holy Spirit, and then go on with their life as if nothing happened? They cap their well. It is not enough to experience the infilling of Holy Spirit and speak in tongues one time at camp or at church. That's not how you tap into the well of the Spirit.

There is a purpose behind the experience. You need to keep being filled…keep being filled. Are you receiving fresh understanding of scripture that arrives with such clarity you find it riveting? Are you more in love with Jesus today than you were last month? Are you concerned, deeply concerned, about lost people? Are you praying for the sick? Are you producing spiritual fruit in your life?

Maybe your answer is something like, "Not like I want. I need more power. I need more love. I need more of God." Then surrender to His will. Pray in the Spirit more. Praise Him more. Meditate on Scripture more. Believe for more. Expect more, even if this process seems to produce no results. Keep praying. Keep believing. Keep on praying in the Spirit, even if you feel stupid. Even when the devil tells you that you are wasting your time, be persistent. "…God rewards those who sincerely seek him." (Hebrews 11:6)

Peacemaker

I love the fact that God is so practical. He wants His love and grace to flow into everything we do, even our relationships. We must uncap the well to allow the flow into our relationships. What happens to our hands when we rub them together fast and hard? They get hot, don't they? But, if we put a little cooking oil in the palm of our hand and then rub them together, our hands don't get as hot. The oil on our skin reduces friction. That's what the oil of Holy Spirit does in families and friendships.

When we allow offense and emotionalism to move into the driver's seat, we miss the opportunity to be a peacemaker. Emotions don't have a driver's license, so don't allow them to drive your actions. Let Holy Spirit drive and guide your actions, even in the most difficult situations. Refuse to become offended, even when you are done wrong. Stay in faith. You do that by building up yourself in Holy Spirit - by praying in the Spirit and calming your emotions with worship. Be a conduit of God's peace wherever you go.

Think about it:
_____

DUI: Dwell Under the Influence

Dear God, What do you want me to take away from this chapter?

Ask for the anointing as you obey the prompting of the Holy Spirit to minister to someone.

Chapter Seven

Power- Electricity

D**ynamo**

"Dunamis" is the Greek word used for power in Acts 1:8. It is pronounced dü'-nä-mēs and means strength, power, or ability. It is used 120 times in the Bible. Let's dig deeper into its meaning:

    a)   inherent power, power residing in a thing by virtue of its nature, or which a person or thing exerts and puts forth

    b)   power for performing miracles

    c)   moral power and excellence of soul

    d)   the power and influence which belong to riches and wealth[88]

Pentecost was the arrival of a living, perpetual dynamo available to every believer. A dynamo is a power generator. People who have experienced tornados and hurricanes understand the value of a generator. Let me explain.

Hurricane Fredrick left Mobile, Alabama, with vast power outages. My parents had two freezers stocked with wild game and garden vegetables, which represented an investment of dozens of hours of hot, hard work, and all of which were irreplaceable this late in the growing season. They scrambled to locate a gas generator to provide power to keep the food in the freezers from thawing and becoming spoiled. Almost everyone in Mobile needed one, so they were sold out everywhere.

Since we lived in Pensacola, FL, they asked if we could locate one. After calling all around, Taylor Equipment promised a truckload of

---

[88]http://www.biblestudytools.com/search/?q=Dunamis&s=References&rc=LEX&rc2=LEX+GRK (accessed June 2, 2011)

generators would arrive at 5:00 that afternoon. We hurried to the store and were third on the list to purchase a generator and waited for the truck to arrive to insure our place in sequence. As soon as we bought the generator, we planned to leave for Mobile. Five o'clock arrived, but the truck didn't. We were hopeful and desperate, so we continued to wait. There were other people in the same predicament that waited as well, which seemed endless as hour after hour crept by. Some of the customers began to leave, including the person whose name was scrawled second on the list, but we were desperate. There was nowhere else to find a generator, so we waited.

It was almost 11 p.m. when the drone of the diesel engine announced the arrival of the generators. As the driver opened the trailer door, we anxiously peered inside the back of the tractor trailer and were shocked to see only two generators. Our name was third on the list. The first customer paid for his generator and drove away. Then, the store manager turned to us, "Mr. Holland, you're the third name on the list. But since the second person on the list is not here and you are, I'll sell this generator to you." Thrilled and anxious, we paid for the generator, loaded it in our car, and hurried to carry power to our family in Mobile.

Back in the upper room, the 120 gathered together and patiently waited. They believed God had more for them and wanted Him desperately enough to wait for Him. They waited until the moment on God's clock, Pentecost, arrived for Holy Spirit to come. Their wait was not as an indicator that we must wait but a measuring tape of their desire and desperation. Samuel Chadwick explains, "The Coronation gift always comes when the King is crowned."[89] Have you crowned Jesus, not just Savior, but King in your life? Have you fallen desperately in love with Jesus? Your deep, sincere worship crowns Him King of Kings. That position of worship and desperation opens the door for you to receive the fullness of Holy Spirit. Obedience and

---

[89]Chadwick, *The Way to Pentecost*; 32.
http://www.raptureready.com/resource/chadwick/chadwick32.html (accessed June 2, 2011)

Pentecost Lost

submission crowns Him King of Kings on the throne of your heart! Crown Him King! No one can worship for you!

As you would expect, our desperate wait for the generator was not because we love or collect generators. We only wanted the power it would bring. Carnal nature approaches God the same way we awaited our generator's arrival: craving the benefits and the power without loving the source of that power. God's kingdom doesn't work that way. Power pursuits constrict the flow of God's power into our lives. God's power flows out of relationship, not manipulation. We should desire, expect to receive, and use the power available to us, but we must never love the power to the exclusion of relationship with Him.

A mobile generator makes it possible to take the benefits of power to places where there is no power. That is one of the reasons God sent Holy Spirit. "Wait," Jesus told His followers. They needed power. They could never accomplish what God had called them to do without Holy Spirit. If they couldn't, then why do we think we can? It is God's plan for every believer to become a distributor of God's love, just like a mobile power plant, bringing light and power to places that need it. This miracle-working power is transforming power, which brings light, love, and life in human jars (clay pots).

Holy Spirit arrived at Pentecost with a complete powerhouse of benefits packaged in His presence. His miracle-working power is available to every believer. Shouldn't we ask ourselves, "Where are the miracles that should be occurring through Christ's modern church"? Have we been robbed by unbelief and religious traditions? Is it enough for us to be fascinated by the events surrounding Pentecost, as a historian traces the history of a significant event or personality? Has the modern church mistaken the Dynamo that God gave believers for a "dinosaur" or "dino," which means fearful[90], and

---

[90]"dinosaur." *Collins English Dictionary – Complete & Unabridged 10th Edition.* HarperCollins Publishers. 05 May. 2011. <Dictionary.com http://dictionary.reference.com/browse/dinosaur>.

which is clearly understood as outdated and extinct and something to be feared? Have we backed away from Pentecost in fear or confusion? Could that relegation - to freeze Pentecost as nothing more than a historical event - cause our culture to spiral downward without knowing the power of a living God? Could it be the reason our churches aren't growing? Could it be the explanation for shriveled and silent believers who should be God's agent of change in this culture? Has wrong information or an erroneous belief system robbed you of Spirit-filled benefits?

Release the Power

Adjectives are inadequate to describe the beauty I experience standing at the base of a waterfall while the spray wets my face and blows my hair. A few adjectives begin to describe what I see and feel: beauty; peace; serenity; awe. Even the trickle of a small waterfall is serene and calming; but, the majesty of a gigantic waterfall is spellbinding and awe-inspiring. Many years ago, wise viewers with an entrepreneurial spirit saw more than beauty; they saw power. Power? Yes, waterfalls are gloriously powerful. Visionaries believed the inherent power in the waterfall could be beneficial. They were not satisfied to view its beauty; they dreamed of releasing its power.

The ancient Greeks developed a simple water wheel, which released the power of falling or moving water as early as 300BC[91]. This hydropower was used to move heavy, grinding stones at gristmills and saws to slice trees into lumber at sawmills. The power that was generated was sufficient to power entire factories. From simple waterwheels to complex water turbines and generators, producing renewable hydroelectric energy, man has captured and used the energy locked in a waterfall.

God is like a waterfall: peaceful; loving; beautiful; majestic; awesome; and, yet, powerful. No one would argue that He is indeed

---

[91] The Perachora Waterworks: Addenda, R. A. Tomlinson, The Annual of the British School at Athens, Vol. 71, (1976), pp. 147-148. Cited at http://en.wikipedia.org/wiki/Watermill (accessed June 2, 2011)

powerful. But, could He share that power with us? Not only could He, He promised that He would. "But when the Holy Spirit has come upon you, you will receive power and will tell people about me everywhere ..." (Acts 1:8)

Is that power accessible to ordinary believers? Absolutely, but it is our responsibility to access it. Prayer is the waterwheel that releases Holy Spirit power into your situation. Prayer is not complicated, but it is essential. There are too many problems in our world, in our government, and in our cities to be content with only indulging in the beauty and majesty of God. It is critical that we see His power released in our lives, so we can touch our neighbors and our community.

Power to Witness

> And when he comes, he will convince the world of its sin, and of God's righteousness, and of the coming judgment. [9]The world's sin is unbelief in me. [10]Righteousness is available because I go to the Father, and you will see me no more. [11]Judgment will come because the prince of this world has already been judged.
>
> -- John 16:8-11

The work of Holy Spirit was to convince the world of three things: its sin; God's righteousness; and coming judgment. The greatest sin is not committing one of the horrendous crimes that earn a person a place on the nation's "Most Wanted List." Instead, it is reliance on personal moral goodness and refusing to believe on Jesus as Savior and risen Lord.

Jesus promised that when Holy Spirit came, He would convince the world of sin. This persuasion is drastically different than the hopeless condemnation used by satan to pound a person. Holy Spirit's urging is tied to the righteousness of a loving God who sent His Son to pay sin's penalty, yet still requiring that redemption be received through faith and repentance. God did not send his Son into the world to condemn it, but to save it. (John 3:17)

Power - Electricity

The Welsh revival of the early 1900's was marked by deep conviction, which caused hundreds of people to repent of their sins and turn to God. It brought a revival that changed entire cities. W.T. Stead said in his book, *The Welsh Revival*, that the men who worked the mines were so changed, that even the mules that were used to work the mines had to be retrained. The miners no longer used profanity, and the mules only understood commands peppered with profanity. Revivals of that magnitude are birthed in prayer. "When He is come ..." When our souls ring out in intercession, He will come. Holy Spirit has come. And He reveals Himself when we pray. Our most desperate desire must be to see the power of God draw people to Jesus. The revival that your city needs must be birthed through prayer. Will you pray? Will you intercede for the lost in your city? Will you pray that Holy Spirit would convict and convince sinners to help them recognize their need to be saved? Will you pray that God will send laborers into the harvest fields?

Holy Spirit works in partnership with believers in the earth. Holy Spirit wants to use each of us to bring lost people to the reality that they need Christ. We must pray, but there's more: we must also witness. Holy Spirit empowerment makes witnessing more effective. We can condemn and contradict, but only Holy Spirit can bring the convincing, convicting power that breaks the power of blindness over a person's life. That's why the convincing work of Holy Spirit is so important. Holy Spirit draws people to Christ when we lift Him up through our testimony and acts of obedience. Through the power of Holy Spirit, you can be a light that reflects the love of Jesus. Ask God to prepare the hearts of unbelievers and give you the opportunity to witness for Him. Ask for boldness, and then step into the opportunities He gives you.

Power of Influence

"The members of the council were amazed when they saw the boldness of Peter and John, for they could see that they were ordinary men who had had no special training. They also recognized them as men who had been with Jesus." (Acts 4:13) The King James Version says "unlearned and ignorant men," which is not exactly the kind of endorsement any ministry seeks. However, it reflects the powerful influence Jesus had on their lives. The world recognized that Peter and John had been with Jesus. His influence, His love, and His power shaped and sharpened these men.

Have you ever surprised yourself by using a favorite expression copied from a close friend? Our society is deluged with cultural influences, from fashion to food choices, dictating the boundaries of what is considered normal. Meanwhile, the believer is considered eccentric when we are influenced by Holy Spirit. You are a new creature with a new capacity to know God. You're not built for the debauchery of sin. As long as you struggle to go back to the old life, you'll struggle in life.

I want to revisit and expand my challenge from Chapter 1 for you to Dwell Under the Influence (DUI). God offers an abundant life that comes only from Dwelling Under the Influence. DUI is more than a once a week church service; it comes from living all of life influenced by Him. It comes from chewing and swallowing the bread of life, the Bible. It comes through conversing with the Father on a regular, ongoing basis. It comes from drinking deeply from the cool springs of Holy Spirit, through worship and praying in tongues. DUI is living life in the warmth of His friendship, influenced by His love, values, and insight.

While Paul was misunderstood and hated by religious people, his words were not empty. He spoke and demonstrated the power of Holy Spirit because he lived under Holy Spirit influence.

> And my message and my preaching were very plain. I did not use wise and persuasive speeches, but the Holy Spirit was powerful among you. ^{5}I did this so that you might trust the power of God rather than human wisdom.
> ---1 Corinthians 2:4-5

Maybe you're thinking that Paul was a preacher, and that kind of power is only for preachers. While the Old Testament limited the

Power - Electricity

anointing to special people, Joel prophesied[92] that the outpouring is for everyone, including you! The world laughs at a believer's powerless prattle. God wants to give us power to both show and tell His love. DUI means His Spirit influences you, like oil seeps into dry skin to soften it or wine influences the reasoning and the senses of its consumer. When you spend time with Holy Spirit, His influence flows into every aspect of your life. His influence changes your desires with the same intensity that maturity and pop trends change what you want. Children dream of riding their bike, but maturity transforms that dream into something with four wheels, like a Ferrari. His influence brings insight that causes us to love the things He loves, and hate the things He hates.

Professor Clark writes:
We may yet employ some such figures as these to denote our sense of the change effected in the disciples by the event of Pentecost. Before this time they believed in Jesus, they were taught and influenced by Him, they obeyed Him; nay, more, they had received great and gracious gifts from Him through Holy Spirit. But now, by the personal descent and manifestation of Holy Spirit, they were in a deeper and more inward manner made to participate in His life; they were drawn into a closer union with Christ and with one another, so as to have a common participation in His risen life, and to be made one body and one spirit with Him. Is it a mystery? Man is a mystery to man and to himself. Truly we may well confess that there is mystery when we think and speak of the things of the Spirit of God, and of the work which He dwells on earth to perform for man on behalf of our risen Lord who is now within the veil.[93]

DUI produces a God consciousness that stirs your faith to believe for results when you pray. Believe God for "Deeds Under the

---

[92] Joel 2:28, 29
[93] Clark, *The Paraclete*, 110.

Influence," including the gifts of the Spirit with signs and wonders, to be His identifying mark on your life. I am convinced there will be few "Deeds Under the Influence" until we learn to "Dwell Under the Influence". "Deeds Under the Influence" was God's plan for the first church, and it remains His plan for the modern church, which includes you. God is looking for people He can reveal His power to and through.

Paul wasn't interested in tickling their ears with fancy words; instead, he wanted to mark their life with the love of God through a demonstration of God's power.[94] Paul could accomplish amazing "Deeds Under the Influence" because he lived his life under the influence. While enduring a horrible storm at sea, Paul shared hope with the men aboard the ship, explaining his peace and resolve with… "For last night an angel of the God to whom I belong and whom I serve stood beside me…" (Acts 27:23) Paul could encourage because he had courage. He could comfort because He had comfort. You can't give what you don't possess.

Pow...er!

The temporary pole erected on the edge of our property was connected to the power transformer the day the construction crew arrived. Every morning, thirteen men poured out of vehicles and scrambled to their position on the construction site. In minutes, the construction site blared with the sounds of electric saws, nail guns, drills, and the drone of air compressors. From time to time, far too frequent to suit the demands of the hard-working crew, the power breaker overloaded. Immediately, the buzz and hum of every electrical tool stopped. "P…ow…er!" they all yelled as if on cue. Elaborate explanations were unnecessary; everyone knew what the "power" yell meant. Long extension cords, coming from all directions, had a single source, the temporary electric pole. When the overloaded breaker popped, the flow of electricity stopped, until

---

[94] 1 Corinthians 2:4-5

Power - Electricity

someone could get to the breaker and reset it. Without fanfare, the worker nearest the power pole rushed to reset the breaker, so construction could continue. Without power, almost everything on the worksite stopped.

The reality is, whether we realize it or not, almost everything of value stops in our lives when the flow of God's power stops. Jesus confessed in John 6:57, "I live by the power of the living Father who sent me; in the same way, those who partake of me will live because of me." His life flows into us, like sap flows through the capillaries of a tree, bringing life and enabling us to be like Jesus in both word and deed.

Within sixteen days, the construction crew stacked the logs, decked the roof, installed the windows, built the porches and interior walls, packed their gear, and left. They were amazing!

They dazzled us with their speed and craftsmanship; none-the-less, we were left with an amazing amount of work to complete. Wayne's next job was to design and install the electrical system in the house. Most blueprints include an electrical plan, but it was not included in this log home package. Local codes mandate where and what kind of outlets and breakers are required. Accurate, up-to-date information is critical to pass the county's mandated inspection. Wayne carefully calculated the circuits and breaker panel requirements. We drilled holes in the 2X4's and pulled the wire bundles from the breaker box through the holes and to the outlet boxes. Every outlet was strategically placed in anticipation of our power needs and lifestyle.

Let me stop here a moment. Strategically plan places where you can plug into God's presence and power. Feed your spirit regularly with more than sweet little verses that makes you feel good or silences your conscience. You need deliberate study habits, such as a daily Bible reading plan that will build your faith and refresh you spiritually. Do you have a specific time and place to pray privately? Do you have a prayer notebook or a file on your computer, where you keep favorite scriptures you use in prayer? Regular church attendance and active participation is the first outlet that comes to most people's

Pentecost Lost

mind. Do you regularly attend a praying church? Are you a spectator or participator in the prayer time? Are you part of scheduled prayer meetings in your church? Some churches have weekday morning or Saturday night prayer times. If you don't have one at your church, organize one in your home.

Let me show you some deliberate prayer outlets that some of my friends have put in place. Maritza said, "The best thing I ever did was to convert that storage room into a prayer room." She added a rug and floor pillows to make the room cozy. It was a place for all her junior leaders to meet for prayer time before they served in children's ministry. That storage room became a strategic outlet for leaders to pray for the service.

Pastor Pete spreads out a big rug for every service, including offsite retreats, so people have a place to pray. It's a lot of trouble, but no one wants to sit or lay on a gym or cold concrete floor. He equips families with skills to have their personal quiet time. Teaching them how to pray is a strategic outlet that encourages everyone to plug in at home on a daily routine.

Karyn's family was trying to buy a house. As a family, they prayed that God's perfect will would be done. They moved forward, confident that this was the house God wanted them to have. Almost daily, a new problem surfaced; daily, they took the situation to God. This situation was a strategic outlet that plugged the entire family into the wisdom and resources of heaven.

Kay was Braden's teacher for two years. He was six now and in a new class. She and her husband were chatting after church with other teachers when Kay saw Braden. She hugged Braden's neck and chatted for a minute, then mentioned to Braden that her husband's back was bothering him. She asked Braden to pray for her husband. He agreed to pray when he got home, but Kay encouraged him to just lay his hand (as she demonstrated for him) on her husband's back and say "Jesus, please heal Mr. Joe." Braden agreed. In simple, child-like faith, Braden began to pray, and then he began to pray in tongues. Kay helped Braden plug into a strategic outlet by encouraging him to pray for her husband. When someone tells you about a need, ask them if they would mind if you prayed for them right then. Praying with them immediately is a strategic outlet that plugs you into the power of God.

110 or 220

The building code now requires that a home be wired with the capacity to handle both 110 and 220 volt circuits. At one time, a house could function with only 110 volt capacity. You can live your entire life in a house with only 110 volt outlets. You can have lights with 110. You can run your vacuum cleaner and the television. You can live life just fine without 220 volt capacity in your home. Of course, you'll have to forget about using your clothes dryer; it runs on 220. You'll need to hang your clothes outside. And you'll need to get used to cold showers because an electric water heater requires 220. Oh, that electric stove requires 220, so you'll need to get used to cold beans and sandwiches. I hope it doesn't get hot where you live because you must have 220 volts to run a central air conditioner. Now, don't miss understand me, those old 110 volt houses are beautiful. Life looks normal from the outside, but if you want to live life to the fullest, you need 220 volts in your home. Why would you want to live without it?

I want to continue with the analogy. You can be genuinely saved and live your whole life without being filled with Holy Spirit; but, why would you want to? Why would you want to live without the fullness of His Spirit?

If you have 220 in your home, your home was wired with a special wire size that is capable of handling that kind of current. Also, 220 receptacles are designed for a specific use. The dryer outlet is especially designed for a dryer plug. The plug on the stove will not fit in the dryer outlet. The experience of the baptism of Holy Spirit wires you to experience the power of Holy Spirit flowing in your life on a regular basis.

My dryer outlet is at the same height as all the other outlets in my house. When I drag my dryer out to clean under it, I have to unplug it. It's frightening to unplug the outlet. I'm hanging over the back of the dryer, and there's almost no room for my arm and shoulder to reach. The big plug is daunting: what if I touch one of the huge, metal prongs? The placement of the outlet makes pushing the plug into the outlet difficult and intimidating!

I will agree that moving in the gifts of the Spirit or witnessing can be intimidating as well! What if I say the wrong thing? What if I make a mistake? What if ... If you're like me, you've made so many "what if" statements. And, let me assure you, you will do the wrong thing, and you will make mistakes - you're human. The disciples did it, and you'll do it. Use wisdom. Serve in the boundaries of love, but don't allow your fear to stop the flow of His Spirit to minister to others.

Conduit Crisis

I wasn't expecting Him to talk to me at that moment. I was listening to my pastor in church when Holy Spirit spoke to my spirit, "There is no energy crisis, only a conduit crisis." He had my attention. I knew immediately He was not talking about the crude oil squabble. As I ruminated over the words, I realized He was reminding me that there is an abundance of the oil of Holy Spirit.

Still, if there is no shortage, then why don't we have more of it? Why don't we have the fruit of the Spirit in our lives? Why don't we see more miracles? Jesus promised they would happen. (John 14:12) Why don't we get along with our families better? Why aren't we making better decisions? Why aren't we experiencing more peace?

Holy Spirit said, "There is no energy crisis, only a conduit crisis." Let's look at conduits. Most cities receive water supplies from large pipes or conduits connected to reservoirs. The Alaska pipeline is a complex system of conduits from the North Slope to the closest ice-free port, Valdez. This amazing conduit is 800 miles long, with oil flowing from the tundra to the port, where it is shipped to refineries.

Wire is a conduit for electricity. Before we started building our home, the power company installed a big, green, power transformer near our property. During construction, we pulled over a mile of wire inside our house. The wire meandered through every room; stopped

Power - Electricity

at every light, light switch, and outlet; and, then we continued to the circuit breakers; but, we had no power. I couldn't even watch television in that house. It was wired beautifully and meticulously, but we didn't have power. There was power available; I could see the transformer from my porch. But, we didn't have it in our house. We wanted power. We needed power. But, we still didn't have it. Why? We were not connected to the source of power.

One day, when all the code requirements were met and the county signed off on its final inspection, the power company came out and connected the power to our log home. Then, we had power! What a day!

In the Old Testament, the miracles and empowerment of Holy Spirit were similar to our temporary power pole put up to supply the power needs of workers until the house was completed. Then, at Pentecost, God sent Holy Spirit to fill any believer, so that through Him,[95] we can connect with God. Although God's transforming power is available to us, somehow we seem reluctant to become a conduit for His Spirit to flow through. We're content to function as a consumer instead of a conduit. This mentality produces the kind of conduit shortage that God warned me about that Sunday morning in church. A conduit crisis results in barren churches and a culture that doesn't know God.

People want to leave it all up to God, but God gave Adam and mankind dominion in the earth. We see the partnership of God with man throughout both the Old and New Testament. God didn't bring a single plague in Egypt without an act of obedience from Moses. I don't understand all the nuances of that partnership, but the reality remains: God's ability flows through the conduits of people. He has established guidelines that dictate the conditions under which His supply will flow. Although it is a simple process, too often it is neglected or ignored. This connection privilege and responsibility are available to every believer through prayer. A believer connects with heaven through prayer, and then faith turns on the valve that releases

---

[95]Ephesians 2:18

heaven's supply. It sounds simple, and it really is, but it also requires tenacity and faithfulness.

As we stay connected, we become a conduit for heaven's resources to flow into the earth. Although the process requires activity and obedience, it is actually a relationship instead of a procedure. Just like Mr. Drake (the innovative oil driller in a previous lesson) had to pound the pipe into the ground to connect with the supply of oil in the ground, prayer connects you to the resources of heaven. As we begin to allow Holy Spirit to flow through us, we will become like gas stations scattered throughout a city. We will be a clay pipeline allowing God's love and God's kingdom to kiss mankind. If we don't clearly understand our role as a conduit, we will not be an available and willing participant.

Potential Power

Theodore Roosevelt said, "It is not what we have that will make us a great nation; it is the way in which we use it." Potential power doesn't produce results, it is when the power is accessed and released that it produces results. You must plug into an outlet to release its power.

The effects of Pentecost didn't stop when that day ended. In Acts 3, Peter and John were going to the temple to pray. A beggar who couldn't walk spotted them and asked for money. Instead of looking the other way, Peter stopped. The conversation went something like this. "Look at me," Peter instructed. "I don't have any money, but I'm going to give you what I do have. Stand up and walk," Peter announced, as he pulled the man to his feet. As the strength flooded into his legs, excitement flooded his heart. No longer could he simply be identified as *the lame man* because now he was jumping and hopping and, perhaps, even dancing. When Peter plugged into the power, God's healing was released in a lame man's body.

I will never forget the first time I was instantly healed. I was sitting on the floor in my baby's room, cradling her, when my little two year old, Jason, climbed on my back. "Oh, Jason, please get off mommy's back. It hurts so badly." I explained.

Jason jabbered back, "I pray for you, Mommy." And he did. Instantly, the pain left me. I was shocked to realize that God could flow through a child that young. God is looking for faith. He flows through people who are willing to plug into His power, regardless of their age or status.

Smoke Alarm

We were trying to eat, but the chirping was so annoying that I just wanted to finish my food and get out as quickly as I could. It was only doing what it was designed to do; the annoying chirp signaled its battery was almost dead. The smoke alarm was begging for attention, and I was ready to beg someone to install a new battery. Its function requires power. It's too late to discover, after a fire, that the battery was dead, so it is wired to chirp when a new battery is needed. A smoke alarm is worthless without power.

God has a plan and a purpose for your life. What you have to give and do is important, but you will never accomplish it without the power of God enabling you. It is not by might, it is not by power, but by His Spirit[96] that you are able to do what He's called you to do. Life with all its demands is draining, so you need power beyond your own.

I wish believers had a warning that would go off when their faith began to run low. I wish we had a built-in reminder to lift our voice to God for more power when our resources begin to drop. Oh, that's right, we do, don't we? It's the inner voice of His Spirit. Don't ignore it. Sometimes there are other, not-so-positive warnings as well: impatience; apathy; frustration; short temperedness; loss of appetite for the Bible and prayer. To a trained ear, each of these chirps becomes a warning that reminds us it is time to recharge our battery.

---

[96]Zechariah 4:6

Pentecost Lost

Pay attention! Is life draining you--get refreshed—plug in! Don't try to pretend you are self-sufficient. You're not! Plug in!

More Effective

It was a beautiful beach, complete with white sand, sparkling blue water, and huge palm trees swaying in the breeze. Relaxing in the shade of a palm tree, we watched a wiry, darkly-tanned man rowing his small rowboat. We were puzzled when the man stopped rowing and lay his paddle down. At first, I wasn't sure what he was doing, but then it surfaced. He was checking his crab pots. He pulled the large crab trap into the boat, dumped the contents into his wet well, lowered the trap back into the water, and then laboriously began rowing again. Slowly, steadily, he rowed. The reality of his labor was intensified as we watched another man roar onto the scene. He shifted the engine to a low rumble, only long enough to retrieve and empty his trap. Then he roared away, quickly disappearing on the horizon, while the first man in his rowboat continued to row.

The difference between the two fishermen was power. One man had only his muscles, while the other had power beyond his ability. Power made that second fisherman more effective, more productive, and wealthier; all those perks come with power. I agree that a boat engine can make a lot of noise, but I prefer the noise to rowing!

My husband was working long hours on his job, so mowing the grass was moved to my to-do list. I didn't mind cutting the grass, but sometimes it grew too tall before I went out to mow it. That made my job really tough, especially since I was using an old push mower.

I was cutting grass on one of those days where the grass was tall and the sun was hot. While sweating and straining to cut grass by my fence, my next door neighbor roared past on his fancy riding lawn mower. Now, I'm known for being frugal. My kids call it stingy, but I call it frugal, so my first thought was, "I could do that, if I was willing to pay the price." Just as quickly as that thought came to my mind, Holy Spirit spoke to my spirit, "And that problem you've been struggling with could be solved if you were willing to 'pray' the price." I understood immediately what He was saying. I needed power - power that He was willing to provide - if I was willing to pay the price of prayer. Why do we struggle in our own strength when God has His surpassing power available to us? My husband never uses a hand saw when the job requires a power saw. It doesn't make sense, does it?

"I pray that from his glorious, unlimited resources he will give you mighty inner strength through his Holy Spirit." (Ephesians 3:16)

Power to Overcome

I was surprised. Snow in Arizona? While it is normal for Flagstaff, it's not what I imagined to see there. As I drove through the cold, blissful beauty, I saw a forest peppered with bare trees -not the deciduous variety that loses its leaves in the winter, but the evergreen, majestic pines. They were stark and naked. Dozens of them completely stripped and more with reddish-brown needles still intact dotted the hillside in dark contrast to their relatives clothed with emerald needles. They were dead giants. Everywhere I looked, I saw fallen giants strewn across the forest floor. Something had shortened the long life spans of these pines. I was puzzled; I had to ask. "What murdered these majestic trees?"

A friendly, knowledgeable, park ranger[97] offered an explanation. Although these trees were thought to be impenetrable, drought had changed the dynamics of the tree's protective system. Without sufficient water, the trees could not produce ample sap to fill the capillaries of the tree. The sap was vital to nourish and stave off intruders. Without adequate sap flowing through the tree, tiny bark beetles, the size of a grain of rice, infested the capillaries of vulnerable trees, killing them. It was hard to imagine that a tiny bug was responsible for devastation of this magnitude. How are the mighty fallen? It seemed that drought and little beetles were the culprits.

---

[97] Walnut Canyon National Monument park ranger

Pentecost Lost

"How are the mighty fallen?" David asked.[98] And I repeat the question to the modern church. Could the culprit be spiritual drought, little sins, little lies, little faith, or little intimacy with God? You can't answer for the Church at large, yet you can stop spiritual drought in your life. Keep the rivers flowing in your life by praying in the Spirit and staying full of God's Word. Deliberately practice biblical processes of daily quiet time in both prayer and Bible study. Stir up your faith, and use it. Stay connected to heaven through prayer, worship, and listening to God. In a climate of spiritual famine, Peter experienced revival because he fanned the flames of his relationship with God. You can, too. Because you are a new creature, sin and wrong habits and wrong attitudes should neither dictate nor intimidate you.

Powerful Prayer

Jesus modeled a life of prayer for us to follow. Facing death and desertion by those He loved, Jesus desperately turned to prayer. Along with His disciples, He made His way to a peaceful grove of olive trees called Gethsemane, away from the distracting noise of crowds.[99] Even the location of His prayer was deliberate; Gethsemane means oil press[100]. As the huge stone crushed and bruised the olives, the olive oil flowed from the press. Here, Jesus submitted His human will to the press of God's plan and purposes. Here Jesus prayed while they slept. Jesus awoke His intimate circle and encouraged them to pray with the warning, "your body is weak." (Matthew 26:41)

Because your flesh is weak and because you are surrounded with temptation, you need the strength that comes from prayer. Release God's power into your life to develop your spiritual muscles. Develop the fruit of self-control, and lean into His nature to become more like Him. Prayer, all kinds of prayer, releases God's power into your life. Yes, there are many types of prayer: the prayer of faith; agreement; petition; repentance; and unknown tongues.

---

[98] 2 Samuel 1:27
[99] Matthew 26:36-46
[100] http://www.biblestudytools.com/lexicons/greek/kjv/gethsemane.html accessed 05/06/11.

Power - Electricity

Have you ever felt worse after you prayed than you did before? I have. I've discovered discouragement comes when I focus on the problem instead of focusing on Jesus--the answer to every problem. Rehearsing a problem repeatedly breeds fear and unbelief that robs our vitality. Take your problems to God in prayer, but release them when you pray. Encourage yourself by praying in tongues; it reminds you that you have a supernatural partnership. So, instead of focusing on the problem continue to pray in tongues, confident that Holy Spirit is praying the perfect will of God through you. Also, you can rest, because you haven't prayed out of your human reasoning. You can release your faith because you know God's best is His will, and you can be confident His will is always best! Do you really trust God enough to be confident that His plan is the best option for you? When you have that confidence, you begin to understand the Father's heart.

A group of girls were strolling down a path when one girl spotted a praying mantis. The skinny, green, stick-looking bug isn't something you see every day, so the girls circled around it, watching as it moved from the folded hand position (that it derives its name from) to a defensive position. Reared up on his hind legs, with his front legs raised defensively, he looked like a boxer. Suddenly, a big bee buzzed onto and snapped the head of the praying mantis right off. The girls ran, squealing. I know this is an alarming picture, but that is exactly what satan wants to do with your faith.

Often we go into God's presence with our petitions, while almost immediately our head gets disconnected. Our mind starts ruminating over all the reasons this problem is too big to handle. While we are analyzing the situation, the enemy is ripping off our faith through fearful thoughts. The battle rages, as we vacillate from faith to fear.

The battle on the fields and plateaus of our mind prompts us to revisit God's strategy of praying in tongues. When we pray in the Spirit, we don't understand what we are saying, so our mind cannot attack the prayer with unbelief. The language is supernatural, and although you don't know what you are praying, God does. From Scripture, we are confident that we are praying the will of God. "And the Father who knows all hearts knows what the Spirit is saying, for

Pentecost Lost

the Spirit pleads for us believers in harmony with God's own will." (Romans 8:27) As we pray His will, He unlocks our faith.

"But you, dear friends, must continue to build your lives on the foundation of your holy faith. And continue to pray as you are directed by the Holy Spirit." (Jude 1:20) The New American Standard reads "But you, beloved, building yourselves up on your most holy faith, praying in the Holy Spirit… " Build yourself up by praying in tongues for all the same reasons you would exercise in the gym: it builds faith muscles like weight resistance develops physical muscles. Working out promotes cardiovascular health, and praying in the Spirit strengthens your heart to love the things God loves and hate the things God hates. Praying in the Spirit causes sin to surface, so you can get rid of it; it is like burning calories stored as unhealthy fat. Praying in the Spirit is an exercise promoting strength and endurance, just like physical exercise.

My membership to the gym didn't benefit me very much because I failed to use it. And, in similar fashion, it's not enough to have a prayer language; it must be used to be beneficial. God has given you the ability to pray in the Spirit for a purpose. When you do, you are praying the perfect will of God. Just like every other prayer, it is a prayer that connects you to heaven's supply.

Before time began, God developed a strategy for every generation that would arrive on the pages of time. His plan includes a detail for every year and every day and how each believer will participate in that plan. That plan is hidden in the heart of God. Precious Holy Spirit searches the heart of God and then helps you to pray that divine strategy with words you don't understand. Holy Spirit helps you pray into existence His perfect will for your life and for others. Our minds can't wrap around the how and the why, but as you pray in the Spirit, you are praying the mysteries of God and bypassing your human intellect. "For if I pray in tongues, my spirit is praying, but I don't understand what I am saying." (1 Corinthians 14:14)

Whether we like it or not, the rules of the kingdom require us to pray if we want to receive. Matthew 7:7 is one of many references that instruct us to ask to receive. Prayer unlocks the resources of heaven.

Power - Electricity

But sometimes we simply don't know how to pray. Sometimes, situations are so convoluted that we have no idea how to unravel it adequately to pray accurately. It's not that we don't want to pray, we just don't know how or what to say. We need help; so God sent precious Holy Spirit to help us. He partners with us to pray the will of God - God's strategy - into the situation. It enables us to pray from God's panoramic viewpoint instead of our hazy, darkened lens.

Knowledge is Power

"As we know Jesus better, his divine power gives us everything we need for living a godly life. He has called us to receive his own glory and goodness! " (2 Peter 1:3) Please don't skip over this verse. Do you realize His divine power has been given unto us, you included, all things...all things, which are needed for life or to make you like God...godliness.

Power is a two-sided coin. We have covered in this lesson the Spirit side of power, but I don't want to close this lesson without flipping to the other side of the coin to remind you that knowledge is power. Wayne was able to wire the house because he had developed the knowledge base, both from experience and studying our county's electrical code. Solomon, a man of great wealth and wisdom, extols the value and benefits of wisdom in Proverbs. I believe God wants to unlock secrets for believers just like He did for King Solomon, Apostle Paul, or George Washington Carver, who revolutionized southern agriculture single handedly.

God has secrets to unlock the energy crisis. My prayer is that He releases it into the hands of Christians who will steward it to bless the world and the Church. God has medical secrets He wants to uncover. Many of our problems have a practical solution instead of a spiritual one. Sometimes changing what you do can save your marriage or help you parent more effectively. Because knowledge is power, it is important to look for and develop skills and knowledge. Ask God to direct you to books and people to help you gain the knowledge you need and to highlight important things for you to recognize.

Pentecost Lost
Think about it:

DUI: Dwell Under the Influence-

Dear God, What do you want me to take away from this chapter?

Do I really believe God's power is available to me? Why or why not?

What is one area I need His power in my life?

Author Info

Why I did it

I was born again as a young child. I loved church, especially testimony time, where I got to talk in church. Even though I was young, I sensed there was something lacking in my life. I went forward at almost every invitation. When I was eleven my Sunday school teacher and a girl that lived down the street from me, began to tell me about the Holy Spirit. I had so many questions, but I was hooked. I wanted all God had for me...I wanted to know the Holy Spirit better. My life-long journey to know Him was launched...and it hasn't stopped. It's been many years...marriage...raising children...ministry...the empty nest...and now the joys of grandchildren. Through all those years God has been faithful and my journey to experience the fullness of the Holy Spirit has increased. I love Him more and realize how little I really know about Him. The more I know Him, the more I want to know.

My second passion has been children's ministry. I had my own children's church when I was fifteen. I've honed and developed my ability to communicate spiritual truths clearly and simply using stories and illustrations to captivate and facilitate learning. In the last five years, my two passions have been combined as my husband and I have ministered to children on the Holy Spirit. It is so exciting to see children receive the Holy Spirit...to see them fall in love with Jesus. That's what happens when we receive the fullness of the Spirit...we fall deeply in love with Jesus. That's because one of the primary jobs of the Holy Spirit is to show, magnify and amplify Jesus to us, so we can know Him better.

Because the children I teach are not children in a church vacuum, I saw the need to expand my vision to include parents and grandparents. I felt the need to include all adults and youth too, because there seemed to be a void; a need to know Him better. People aren't generally filled unless they know God has more for them. I wanted to see more believers filled to overflowing with Him and all the benefits His relationship brings. I am convinced God hasn't changed His mind regarding the church. We just need to access His ability in order to live out those virtues. So, that's why I wrote the book.

I wrote the book because I want you, your family and your friends to "always triumph through Christ." I want you to experience the fullness of God, the love of God and the communion of the Holy Spirit.

This book is not a theological exegesis, but it is a journey through scripture to help the reader fall in love. This book is written in a clear, easy to understand format using seven words pictures that describe Holy Spirit. It uses interesting stories from nature and history to unlock the mystery of Pentecost. This book is for the person that doesn't know anything about the Holy Spirit. It's for the person that avoids the whole conversation because they think it's all weird. And it is also for anyone who has received the Baptism of the Holy Spirit but wants to rekindle their passion, or wants to know how to access the resources available to the Spirit filled believer. You will be inspired and ignited. You will fall in love—all over again.

This book is written to pastors or leaders that need a little extra help making the whole topic of receiving the Holy Spirit easier to understand. It gives clear examples and illustrations that can be used in conversation, training and sermons.

We will be releasing DVD sessions for Sunday School, small groups or week night training times. We also plan to release a children's ministry curriculum so the entire family can learn about Holy Spirit at the same time.

Author Info

About Pat Holland

First, I'm a child of God, and I love Him with all my heart. I am a passionate believer who takes the Word of God literally and purpose to live every area of my life under the influence of His Word and His presence.

After 40 years of marriage, I am still ardently in love with my husband. Every time he walks into the room, my heart skips a beat; no pace maker can fix that. He is a precious man who loves God. We love to work together, and we are a great team. We cook, pray, walk and build together. I have held the dumb end of more boards than I can count! That's another story for another day.

We have two precious children and 4 grandchildren. I can't afford to start talking about them, because I would bore you to tears with the details. I love, love being a Nana and a mother. They are treasures from God and I value them more than I can express to you.

I am a minister with the Assemblies of God. I preach, teach, and write. My passion is to make the Bible come alive so people can walk out its principles in their everyday life through the power of the Holy Spirit. I love meeting people and getting to pray for them and with them. My motive gift is encouragement and it ebbs into everything I do. I've been honored as the keynote speaker for International, statewide and local conferences. I am passionate about the things of God. I crave and pursue His wisdom and anointing.

I became involved in children's ministry when I was fifteen years old. I love preaching to kids. I have found that kids love the presence of God. Children love to hear anointed preaching, as long as it's not too long, and they can be filled with the Holy Spirit. I am so excited about the move of the Spirit that I am seeing in children.

But, children are not raised in a church vacuum. They are influenced by their parents and older siblings. And, because there seems to be confusion and concern in many full-gospel churches on the when and how surrounding receiving and experiencing the fullness of the Holy Spirit, many believers are left in the dark without the benefits God intended them to have. That is alarming! Jesus sent

Pentecost Lost

Holy Spirit to be His active agent in the earth. Without Him we lack the resources to be the overcoming believers God intended.

Pentecost is not a place, a church-thing or a relic from the past. Pentecost is the fulfillment of God's promise to send a helper; someone to come along beside every believer to help them know God better, and out of the life that flows from relationship, live overcoming lives that influences others. I want to inspire you to know precious Holy Spirit more deeply with this book, *Pentecost Lost*. I hope you'll read it, share it and give it to a friend. Use it in a Bible Study. Mark the pages. Ask Holy Spirit to reveal Himself to you in a fresh way in every chapter.

I pray God's blessings on you and your journey to know God more deeply.

Follow my blog at **www.patriciaholland.org/blog**

Look for the release of Pentecost Lost small group and children's ministry curriculum at: www.patriciaholland.org